SUPERIOR VOYAGE

SUPERIOR VOYAGE

Ten Year Anthology

The Marquette Poets Circle

edited by

Richard J. Rastall

ISBN: 978-0-9857127-6-1

Cover photographs by Richard J. Rastall

Dedication

This book is dedicated to:

Genean Granger (1943 – 2019)

and

Bert Riesterer (1935 – 2018)

The Marquette Poets Circle

The Marquette Poets Circle is open to everyone. The Marquette Poets Circle was created by Matt Maki, Claudia Drosen and Janeen Pergrin Rastall to encourage and inspire writers of all experience levels. For more than a decade, the Poets Circle has held workshops, Open Mics and readings. They have collaborated with Peter White Public Library and the City of Marquette Arts and Culture Center on events and projects including the Sidewalk Chalk Poetry Contests and the Mad Poets Tea Party. During the pandemic, the poets created "Hearts to Hearts, 2020 Pandemic Literary Project" (words shared with the UPHS Staff), and participated in the Marquette Memory Box podcasts. For the 2021 Art Week, the Poets Circle performed Opening, Closing and Pop-up readings and a "Stump the Poet" challenge. The public has been encouraged to experience the convergence of poetry and visual art in the MPC exhibits at Peter White Library's Huron Mountain Gallery, Lower Gallery, and the Travel Marquette Gallery. In 2020, the poets created an interactive exhibit, "Words and Music" collaborating with Borderland Arts of Iron Mountain which was displayed in the Huron Mountain Gallery. In October 2021 the poets created an exhibit, "Herstory, the Women Who Inspire Us" at the library. In 2021, the Marquette Poets Circle was named the 2021 Community Arts Organization by the City of Marquette. The Marquette Poets Circle is a member of the Poetry Society of Michigan and the National Federation of State Poetry Societies.

Superior Voyage: 10 Year Anthology

This anthology features 42 contributors. The contributors to this anthology include: 2 former Upper Peninsula Poet Laureates, 3 City of Marquette award winners for writer of the year, poem and book award winners, authors of many published books, 2 publishers, multi-talented artists, 2 ministers, current and former English Professors, 2 former Artists in Residence at Isle Royale National Park, 1 person who has lived in Ukraine since the Russian invasion in 2014 and many contributors with diverse educational backgrounds and employment. Many of the contributors chose short bios omitting several of their accomplishments.

Gordon Publications published *Maiden Voyage – The Marquette Poets Circle Five Year Anthology* in 2018. In a "Marquette Monthly" review, Tyler Tichelaar said:

"*Maiden Voyage* may well be the most significant volume of poetry ever published in Upper Michigan".

Lakestruck

We can hear the lake,
we can wade the shallows, bend in the quiet
and discover Superior's history.

She breathes out memories:
sunsets cast across ice floes,
the distance a broken pine tree floats.
She croons about all she carries:
moon glimmer, cast off freighter lights,
sturgeon and whitefish dreams, skeletons
of all that sank. She sings of what she holds close
and what she lets go. Water she's kept
since 1830, she feeds down the St. Mary –
a fresh gift to lesser lakes while our decades
of discards await.

She curtsies - a toss of froth and foam.
Kick your shoes off, bow and tiptoe
forward then back. Like a toddler,
meet each wave, then laugh and retreat.
On this beach, with this blue, this clear beauty,
you can cheat death for a bit.

Janeen Pergrin Rastall

An earlier version of this poem appeared in *What Does Water Mean To You,*
a City of Marquette Art Week Publication (2022).

CONTENTS

GIDEON ACHATZ

Yeti's Fish

Yeti sits with his spear,
waits for fish.
He waits and waits,
tries to spear. Misses.
For weeks.
Sees other yetis rarely,
accepts starvation.

Lady Yeti taps his shoulder.
He almost kills her from fear.
She carries a doe, drops it
in front of him.
He digs into it.
Wild, sloppy.
He finishes the doe, gives
her a bloody hug.

He continues to fish.
Every three weeks,
she comes back with food.
More deer. A grizzly bear
on Christmas and his birthday.
He finally catches a sturgeon,
tries to find her. But he is old.
Doesn't get far.
Falls to the ground.
He feels a tongue on his cheek,
looks up. It's her. He flips, motions
for her to take the sturgeon.
She accepts it, eats it,
stays with him to the end
of his breath.

Lady Yeti buries him, digs deer antlers
into the ground to mark he once was.
She still visits every three weeks.
Brings a doe. When she returns
three weeks later, it is always gone.
No yeti tracks, no blood.
Just a fresh sturgeon,
waiting for her in the snow

Yeti Christmas

Snow falls on an Australian shepherd's nose.
Wreaths spread pine needles everywhere.
Cold, freezing cold, sub-zero.
Just how he likes it.

He creeps around windows on Christmas Day.
Watches kids bloom with happiness
as they rip open presents
like they are predators,
the presents, their prey.

Then Yeti walks back to his snow cavern.
Old Mother Yeti sits inside,
skinning a buck. Its antlers
scratch her arms. She gets up,
hugs Yeti, kisses his forehead.

Old Mother Yeti motions to the deer,
famished. A pine needle falls
on Yeti's head. He looks up.
Mistletoe hangs above him.

They sit together,
share this Christmas feast.

Honey

The thick gold sticks on.
Bumblebees all work today.
Now it rests ever.

Life is Like . . .

We got the best box of chocolates.
Brown eyes like Willy Wonka's chocolate river.
She was a rose bush,
thorny, always beautiful.

She planted seeds in every person,
her kindness blooming the best day
when they talked to her.

Aunt Rosey was a gift.
The lost piece of the puzzle.
The painter of a cherry blossom.
The surf on the waves.

I hope God gives her
the best place in heaven,
with as many latch hooks
and Diet Cokes as she wants.
Where every night, she gets
mashed potatoes and
Kentucky Fried Chicken
for dinner.

Jim Rummy

Jim Rummy with her was one of the best
parts of both of our days. She was polite,
understood that I was a child.
She didn't always know who I was,
but I loved watching her
wrinkled hand take a card.
She had mahogany eyes,
glasses that rested on her
shell ears. Her hair was
white poplar, her face smooth
as butterfly wings.

I would pick up the deck, shuffle cards.
I crave that noise to this day.
I placed the cards on the table,
let her pick first. I picked my card
after her. We didn't ever care about runs
or pairs. Sometimes she forgot
how to play, and I helped her. That warmed me,
could warm me even if I was in the arctic.
It didn't matter who won.
It was just for fun. For love.

I imagine her up in heaven now,
shuffling the deck. Dealing the cards.
Playing Jim Rummy with grandpa.
Of course, grandma always wins.

MARTIN ACHATZ

Bigfoot Meets a Homeless Man on Presque Isle

The man smells wild,
the way a black bear smells
after winter sleep, full
of hunger, dizzy from
root and dark. Bigfoot can taste
loneliness on the man, a sweaty
slick of days spent near
the big water, hidden in pine,
rooting through garbage cans
for leftover French fries, brown
apple cores still sweet and seeded,
hot dog buns gone chlorophyll green.

Bigfoot knows
this man will die soon,
has seen it before when moose
with brain worm stumble off
by themselves, or one eaglet shreds
a feebler eaglet to get
more perch and salmon from
their mother's beak. Even this close
to lights and cars and houses, survival
is all about being bigger, stronger,
hairier, scaling trees for nested
eggs, scooping silvery spottails from Superior
surf, tearing haunches off mewling fawns.

Bigfoot wants
to help the man who has wandered
onto this rocky thumb surrounded by wave.
Wants him to feel wanted
as soft leaves or a run of smelt.
As the man beds down for the night
under a ribcage of branches, Bigfoot
knuckles one tree trunk, knocks, knuckles
again, knocks. He does this until
he hears hollow, then scratch, chatter.
He plunges his hand into the tree,
extracts a panicked squirrel.

Bigfoot snaps
its neck like a cricket leg. Holds
the carcass to his chest, breathes the last
pulses of its pebble heart, then grunts
an ape prayer of thanks, a sound
like a mother giving birth under
a blazing comet to something
necessary. Needed.

Bigfoot leaves
the squirrel at the man's sleeping
feet, where he'll find it in morning
light. An offering of meat, blood, fur.
To remind the man that the world
loves him.

Ascension
for Rose, February 5, 2022

I wonder what Jesus did as he ascended
on that elevator of cloud. Did he wave
to the disciples as he rose and rose
like some kite broken free of its string,
becoming smaller, smaller until he
was swallowed by the great blue
throat of heaven? And did the disciples
keep their eyes trained on him,
unblinking, until tears transformed
that mountaintop into the Sea of Galilee?
After he was gone, did the disciples stand
there, look at each other dumbly, try
to recall his last word? Was it
earth or *dirt* or *air* or *mother*?
They didn't have phones to take
pictures or videos. Weren't able to
scroll through their albums
to remind themselves how dark
his skin and eyes were or how
laughing made him blaze
like Pentecost. Instead, they gospelled
each other, tried to recall with letters
God's whiskered face.

Today, we gather
in this church for you, dear sister, two
weeks after the metronome of your lungs
ceased and you ascended on that cold
morning. I stood by your bed, held
your hand, mapped its pulse
with my fingertips. I don't remember
the last word you spoke to me,
or even second to last. It may
have been my name or *mother*
or *ham* or simply *yes*. Like the disciples
now, I'm greedy for every
last scrap of you, your crooked
smile, how you cackled even
when you didn't get the joke. I
spent my entire life knowing
you, but not really knowing.
Until the end, when you were
rising and rising away from me,
getting smaller, smaller. I
watched until you vanished
from sight, taken back
to that place you came
from, that infinity between zero
and one. Only then did I realize
how lucky I'd been. To have
you with me every day, drinking
Diet Cokes, listening to ABBA
songs, begging me to wrap
my arms around your
shoulders. I could spend the rest
of my days writing gospels and gospels
about how much you loved me.

The Quiet Man

Last night, I dreamed my dad and John Wayne
were sitting around a campfire, eating
peaches out of a can. Stars thick as cattle herds
milled above them, and the prairie grass
hummed some sweet old song like "Red River Valley"
or "Shenandoah." I'm not sure if it was heaven,
but my father was young and perfect, the hook
of his back as straight as a railroad spike.
Duke was young, too, the retired prizefighter
who chased Maureen O'Hara through the green
Galway countryside. There weren't any Nazis
crawling along the ground in ambush, no
Richard Boone-faced kidnappers, skin
leathery as buffalo jerky, trying to steal
their sleeping horses. I'm not sure
if you can smell in dreams, but I remember
smelling manure and smoke and something else.
Maybe the coming of rain. My dad and Duke
didn't talk, just forked golden crescents
into their mouths, looking as if they were eating
solar eclipse after solar eclipse. Their forks
made hollow cowbell noises in the dark.
When they were done, they tipped the cans
to their lips, drank the syrup inside
until it ran down their chins. I kept
waiting for something more to happen,
a runaway stagecoach to crash through
or a baby elephant nosing for hay.
Instead, my dad took a deck of cards
from his pocket, started dealing.
They played gin rummy, hand after hand.
My dad let John Wayne win, because he was
John Wayne and because that's what
my dad did every morning with my mother
for years and years. He did it because
it was a habit of love. Maybe that's the name
of this movie: *Habit of Love*. It starts out
simply enough. Two cards. Dealt face up.
The king and queen of hearts.

Doe After a Blizzard

My son noticed her first, splayed, bloody, broken by a neighbor's fence.
A dead doe, shining in the sunlight that always comes after a blizzard,
sunlight so strong it hurts to step into it. Sunlight that shouts.

The doe was haloed in that light, and my son, only five, said,
Fix it, daddy, reduced me to an Easter Island carving, stone face
immutable in the presence of suffering. I wanted to tell my son
I can't or *She's gone* or *She's with God* or some other
emptiness recited in church every Sunday so often that it has lost
its ability to comfort. Instead, I picked my son up, carried him
closer to the doe, whispered in his ear *Isn't she beautiful?*

I watched his face change, confusion give way to something
seraphic. *Yes*, he said, nodding. *Yes, she is. Yes. Yes. Yes. Yes.*

Can I Tell You?

Can I tell you that you were beautiful in your hospital bed, with your dark hair oiled to your face? Can I say that your chapped lips parted, and air bubbled between them in tiny hiccups, and that was beautiful, too? Can I mention the sound of the IV beside you, beeping, pinging like a tiny railroad crossing, how beautiful that noise was? Can I say how I sat beside you and held your hand as you slept, and even the smell of you was beautiful--the sweat and stale breath and gas coming from your body? And the sour sweetness of breast milk rising from your nightgown, how it filled me with layers and layers of onion contentment. Peel away a layer. Contentment. Peel away another layer. More contentment. Can I tell you all this now, so many years later? Can I remind you of the happiness we had that day, that night, as the sun went down on our son's first hours of breath? How I didn't know that moment, holding your hand, watching you sleep, was one of the best moments of my life? If I had only known. If I had only known.

ERIN ANDERSON

Mining a Summer of Pain and Pleasure in the UP

During one American summer break from working overseas, I rented an upstairs room in Michigan's Upper Peninsula in a friend's divorce house, as she called it. Using the proceeds from her settlement, she'd purchased a house built by an iron-mining company. The lot was large enough for a vegetable garden and a clothesline that women no longer had to swipe clean of ore dust before hanging laundry. But a coating remained, expelled by the furnace of my friend's abandonment rage.

I did my best to dispel it. I turned up the radio on Sunday mornings while I baked bread. I re-arranged and tended her houseplants. I categorized her books and read them. I pulled video tapes out of their sleeves and watched them. I dusted off her knick-knacks and draped a lace curtain over her high-top piano to hide exposed sinews. I organized the raw materials of her life.

Then a man in his forties who lived with his mother on a neighboring lot invited us to visit his family's camp on a spring-fed lake. He seemed harmless. He was polite. He had suffered his entire life from a congenital defect at the base of his spine, but he was still able to do janitorial work at the Lutheran Church across the main road. He blamed his defect on the fact that his mother was forty when she'd given birth to him, but I wondered if mining toxins had leached into her system.

My friend turned down his invitation to swim in the nearby lake, but I accepted. And to press home the point that you should enjoy what you had, I made a habit of it. All summer, the neighbor man and I splashed and played like little kids, squinting in the sunlight, the minnows teasing our toes as we dangled and dipped from the dock. That was the summer I thought of myself as sixteen again, as a virgin whose biggest responsibility was to hang out with her friends.

I did not know that the neighbor man had a scar in his esophagus from drinking vodka. I did not know that he had not had a drink in two years, only starting again after I told him I was not going to marry him, after which he got so drunk, he fell down his mother's stairs. I did not know that mining my pleasures could result in the collapse of another's.

Toward the end of the summer, my friend exploded in a rage the afternoon I pulled a patio umbrella out of the shed and scrubbed it clean because the vinyl umbrella had belonged to her dead grandmother. Then she raged when the neighbor man mowed her lawn because she'd wanted all the wildflowers to grow. It was time for her to take back the organization of her life. It was also time for me to return to my life across the Atlantic.

Within a year, my friend put her house up for sale and relocated to a more populated area of Wisconsin where she was able to extract the resources important to her: a job and a mate. The neighbor man also made changes to his life. He got a computer and started chatting with people on line where he could communicate without worrying about his hand tremor, which he had tried to suppress with alcohol as a teen. Not longer after his mother passed away, he followed, finally safe from any further excavation of his pain.

A Covert Miracle Worker

I first observed the covert nature of miracle work in graduate school, where it was clear that my English professors were impostors. They had to be. They had to mask their true motives with secret codes, convoluted theories, and artificially elevated diction. They hid behind a facade of "science" to conceal their mission, which was nothing less than miraculous.

When I joined their ranks, I donned my disguise. I wore long skirts and tailored jackets and jewelry that was just shiny enough. Armed with red ink, I marked up my students' papers as though what mattered most were the ten rules for comma use, but that was a ruse to divert attention away from the essays I had written about my life, about incest and the excitement of buying a Polish-English dictionary in a medieval town. I even told them I had had a venereal disease, one I suspected some of them might be carrying.

My true mission was confession. That was the miracle that lanced shame, and many followed suit, baring their souls, but not all. One student wrote all of his papers on golf, but since he was able to correctly place his punctuation and identify his rhetorical mode, he got an A.

Then I joined the Peace Corps and went to the former Soviet Union, where we were already considered foreign agents of soft power bent on destroying entrenched patriarchies with perverted Western values. That was not far off the mark. Those goals, however, were not stated in our handouts, which were craftily encoded with a global model to be applied everywhere, but too general to be applied anywhere.

Despite the rubrics and check lists and objectives and evaluation criteria, miracles abounded. I spent nearly a decade in the Peace Corps, working in four Former Soviet Republics. Myself and everyone who crossed my path were mutually infected, repeatedly, in spite of ourselves, with language and cultural values and questions about who we were and our purpose on this planet. Miracles struck whenever human beings told their stories.

Government Guilt

Three years after 9/11, an Arizona high school pulled out of an exchange program in Central Asia. The American coordinator said parents did not want to send their children to Kazakhstan because of the war in Iraq. The disappointment here in this Eastern Kazakhstan city of 320,000 led to such remarks as "Kazakhstan isn't even near Iraq!" When I pointed out that a bomb in neighboring Uzbekistan might be to blame, the local coordinator thought another geography lesson was in order because "We're way up in the east." And she was right. This was a huge country--the ninth largest (after Russia, Canada, China, US, Brazil, Australia, India, and Argentina). And what with the roads periodically missing chunks of pavement, distance expanded between us and the more chaotic countries to the south. But I didn't think the American parents needed a geography lesson. I thought they needed to understand that in this ostensibly Muslim country with an official language of Turkic origin, this eastern city of Ust Kamenogorsk, at least for now, was heavily Russian. Most of the schools still taught in Russian. Most of the teachers were Russian. Five or ten years down the line, if they didn't learn Kazakh, what would happen to them here? That was why the more contacts with Americans, representatives from arguably the most successful country on the earth, the better.

These Russians believed in American success. And as an American, I was expected to deliver the recipe for a successful life. If I could, I was sure the English teachers I worked with would memorize it and then force all their students to memorize it. But even in their hearing of it, they would filter it through cultural expectations--that the social system itself, headed by a strong leader, was supposed to be strong, inflexible and responsible for quality of life. "If Stalin were around today, he'd know what to do with terrorists. He'd kill the terrorist's whole family. Heck, he'd kill the whole village."

Russians did not suffer from government guilt. When they were exposed to newly released information about Russian oppression of Kazakhs, for example, they rejected it. When they heard that "harsh measures taken to separate the Kazakhs from their horse and sheep and to move them into reeducation camps resulted in near-genocide," they said things like, "Russians didn't oppress Kazakhs. In history, things just happen." And maybe things did just happen, with the "best" of intentions, that road to hell with better pavement than a Kazakh highway. How could a nomadic people really understand what settlements would bring? How could they know what empire meant? And why should subjects of a totalitarian empire feel any guilt for the actions of its leaders?

I was reminded of my grade school lesson on smallpox-infected blankets. I remembered my horror at such a lethal trick, and maybe a little awe at such diabolical cleverness. But as a citizen of a democracy, what was I supposed to do with that information? Vote for politicians devoted to reparations? Or simply recoil from the bad feeling of it? And I continued to flee the enormity of my implied responsibility, my American guilt. I felt guilty for reaping benefits from a capitalist system that propelled some to such amazing material success while it ground up others. I felt responsible for the mistakes of my government, for the behavior of my elected officials, even if I did not vote for them. I should have done more, campaigned harder for the opposition, knocked on more doors, handed out more pamphlets. My paradox as an American was to feel responsible for the behavior of other Americans whom I could not control, Americans who were really quite ordinary, fallible, sometimes quite ignorant. This American guilt complex anticipated punishment. And that fear of anti-American reprisal was probably what prompted those parents to keep their teenagers in their Arizona suburb.

But if I tried to explain this to the locals, if I tried to say, "We are afraid you don't like us," this would be met with disbelief because both Russians and Kazakhs here loved Americans, filling my glass, heaping my plate. They would never think that the woman before them was responsible for bombing Iraq--silly thought. (Although, as a "wealthy" woman, I was responsible for giving my money to the poor and needy because justice meant that everyone had the same amount of stuff.) They understood that the world was a confusing place. Life was unpredictable. That was why our glasses were raised often with heartfelt wishes, incantations of hope for health, happiness, and always, success.

(Published in *The Mississippi Review* in 2004.)

American Streets

On a suburban street, a neighbor mowed past his yard, shaving wild grasses in sandy soil, carving a huge expanse to be tended. He lifted up his entire garage, moved it over several yards, and began building a sun porch. Before construction was complete, he entered the psych ward. Then his wife left him. A tumult of asphalt in a dug-up driveway marked the destruction of this family. My marriage had fallen in on itself, not in a suburb, but on a country road, where a lacing of cracks reappeared on the plaster walls and spinachy patches of goose droppings from the bottom of our shoes marred the painted floor. I ran away from decaying linoleum and an architect of multi-storied dreams.

In my box of tan and brown, in one of 32 apartments, no sliding glass door, no window box, no balcony, I was invisible, not like my neighbors in their single-family dwellings, their every shrub and lawn ornament a declaration of class and taste and personal habit. No one saw my tastes, my shame, in my cluster of cubicles where I nourished, rested, escaped. It was where I organized my thoughts for public consumption, the most interior parts of my being craving display.

Concrete boxes housing reasonably-priced goods filled my vision as I walked in the drizzling rain. I hated these business-loop, U.S.-freeway sections, their flat, broad roofs, their asphalt moats, tolerated by citizens zipping by in cars. So I went back to Central Europe, to corner turrets and canted roofs and onion-domed spires, where buildings had faces. Art-chitecture. Pretty stuff with no purpose. I smuggled these images inside of myself. I became a corner turret, like the Italian professor at the university who was born in Rome. "I'm proud to be from Rome. I'm an ambassador for its culture." He thought he was the freaking Coliseum. Then I remembered I was not a building. And when I returned to America, I no longer looked for artistry where none had ever been professed.

I walked the stories of Midwestern streets, starting at the downtown bus depot, where beginnings were boarded and broken. The story picked up in the middle with a charity office, a Hooter's, an adult bookstore, but the happy ending was the main thing in America, the climax at river's edge, a riverboat casino, a jogger's path, or a 630-foot arch of steel and hope and a nationally recognized hotel where I had brunch. I turned around and walked back, back to dereliction, back to a failure that stung because of all that had been promised.

(Published in Word Riot in 2005.)

The Need for Neighbors

When I was ten years old, my divorced father fantasized about fleeing the prying eyes of neighbors. He talked about the Amazon rain forest or a beach in Mexico, but the only place my mother let him take me and my brothers was the Uintah Mountains in Utah where our neighbors were coyotes, campers, and a clever game warden who dumped hatchery fish off a bridge near our campground. We caught them before the throbbing knot of flailing fins untangled themselves. The next morning all the other fathers were sober enough to leave early. Then the game warden paid us a visit and casually asked, "How many'ja get?" and my brother said, “Sixty-two,” so we were escorted into the small mountain town. My grandmother wired the $300 fine. My father's subsequent shame subdued his drinking enough to get us back home.

In 1971 a fifty-something-year-old man was entrusted with three eleven-year-old girls in the back country of California's Yosemite National Park because our divorced mothers were too overwhelmed to think about it much. My teacher taught us how to wear a large backpack, unhooking the belt when we crossed a river so that if we fell in the water, the pack would not pull us down. He showed us how to cook dehydrated food in metal coffee cans. He showed us how to spot stacks of rocks that signaled where the trail crossed granite. He showed us how to set up pup tents in which we waited out the afternoon rain showers. This was how children learned problem-solving skills and thus gained self-confidence.

I hiked with him while the other two girls lagged behind. Then it got dark. He said we should set up camp. He told me not to worry. He would notify the ranger about the girls in the morning. He was the adult. Of course he was right.

We took off our backpacks, and he started a fire. I began to rub my sore shoulders. He took over the job, kneeling behind me, his hands pressing into the flesh, but I pulled away.

He seemed irritated. His hands returned to my shoulders, becoming insistent. "This will relax your muscles," he told me.

The backpack straps had worn my skin raw, and he was making it worse.

Other campers set up nearby. I pulled away again. He backed off. Thank God for neighbors.

The girls arrived at our campsite the next morning. They were also grateful for neighbors--the camping family who had fed them.

Our trip continued peacefully, the only danger coming from a lack of calories our final morning because while we slept, a bear pulled down the bag of food we had hung on a tree branch. When I remembered this trip later as a teenager, I was struck by this bear's culinary fastidiousness, how it had eaten everything except the dehydrated green beans and potato soup. As an adult, I was struck by my teacher having abandoned two eleven-year-old girls in bear country.

My band director and choir teacher, a man whose cologne I would later recognize as remarkably similar to vodka, wanted to take his students away from their neighbors. He planned to take a select choir on a road trip to Mexico. This man was also living with the eighteen-year-old drum majorette who had graduated the previous year and was not going to college, about which her parents were quite upset. I auditioned by singing "To Dream the Impossible Dream" from *Man of La Mancha*, and then I did not hear any more about it. They went on the trip without me. When they returned, I heard he'd called late-night rehearsals during which all of the teenage girls had worn their nightgowns

.

When he saw me at school, he asked, “Why didn’t you come with us?”

My mother, not too overwhelmed at this point in her life, must have torn up the permission letter, saving me from his ogling and a failed career as a lounge singer.

When I was nine years old no man wanted to remove me from the prying eyes of neighbors. He didn’t have to. He was my grandfather, and all he had to do was be alone with me in the house.

(Published in *Bending Genres* 2019.)

Sickled O'er with the Pale Cast of Milk Chocolate

When my father died in his sleep from myocardial infarction, my brother blamed me. He accused me of driving the sugar train that had run him over. My brother happened to be suffering from schizophrenia, but that did not mean he was mistaken. I had driven the sugar train. Sugar had been a major ingredient in our bonding. I had been only too happy to run out to the store and buy a Sara Lee cheesecake on a Sunday afternoon so that my father and I could eat it while we watched television. We were simultaneously comforted by the predictable sweet creaminess and the predictable television narratives. We were safe from the intrusion of my brother's worsening ramblings.

A few days after my father died, I saw him in a dream. "I thought you died," I said.

He silently shrugged his shoulders.

"Well, we're going to have to watch your diet so that doesn't happen again!"

Much later in life, I discovered that my own body was having a hard time metabolizing sugar. Insulin resistance they called it. So I finally committed to decreasing my intake, but then I began to notice a social plot to keep me heavily sugared. Sitting in a buffet-style cafeteria with friends, I admired a piece of cake that was destined to be consumed by a man in our group. “That looks good,” I said. It was just an innocuous comment during a lag in conversation, but one of the women got up, went to the dessert island, and returned with a pink frosted square. She put it by my plate. This was not her home, and I had not asked for a piece of cake. I had simply remarked on the attractiveness of a dessert about to be eaten by her diabetic husband.

When I was working in an elementary school in Armenia as a Peace Corps Volunteer, the social forces that encouraged the intake of simple carbohydrates took on cult-like proportions. Many ate nothing for breakfast beyond a small cup of coffee, taking sips between bites of chocolate. The teachers also had no regular lunch. Sometimes they ate sweet buns. Other times they tore chunks of white bread off a flat loaf and ate it with salty cheese, but usually no regular sustenance was ingested beyond serial sips of coffee and bites of chocolate during school hours. Even when I politely refused a chocolate, my counterpart unwrapped it and placed it next to my coffee cup. Later I found out that her father had had a diabetes-related foot amputation. When I saw an article in Armenian detailing the evils of white flour, explaining how it raised blood sugar levels, I brought it to school and forced several of my colleagues to read it. Other Americans used their language skills to form life-long friends. I used mine to lecture and annoy.

I occasionally relapsed. After ducking into the Moscow Cinema in the capital city of Yerevan to watch a Russian-dubbed American action film, I sat in the back row and scraped melted Jumbo Twix chocolate off the inside of the wrapper with my teeth. This was my escape from a life that overwhelmed. Besides, it was the *weekend!* I was supposed to be having fun and not be psychologically weary from listening to Armenian educators scream at children all week. After yelling during the first few weeks of school, one teacher lost her voice.

I had listened to enough screaming in my life. As my brother's schizophrenia bloomed during his teenage years, my alcoholic father increased his rants, calling my brother the worst things possible in the English language. About ten years later, my brother would follow my father to the grave. It was interesting that my brother had used a train metaphor when referring to what he perceived as my culpability in our father's heart condition because it would be a train that my brother would use to end his own life. There wasn't enough sugar or chocolate or white bread to help me with that.

(Published in Oxford Magazine in 2020.)

ESTHER MARGARET AYERS

My Paper Map

for Dan

Today I ironed my paper map: it's a map
of Michigan's Upper Peninsula, my home.
I like living with water on almost every side
because I myself am mostly water. They're
not making maps like this much anymore;
most people prefer using GPS. I see them in SUVs
or on trails staring at those tiny screens or else
looking angrily at the sky when there's no signal.

I like my paper map, wrinkled from so many journeys.
It reminds me of my lover's face, of love's body,
love's worn jeans and flannel shirt. We've laid this map out
on flat rocks at the bottom of the Sturgeon River Gorge,
the beach near the mouth of the Laughing Whitefish
and the hot hood of our truck, the engine ticking as it cools.
We've spread it out on tent floors, motel beds, boat bows,
bars and picnic tables. On my map St. Mary's straits
are blurred from raindrops and there are double rings
in Lake Superior where we rest our coffee mugs.

Even so, today I ironed my paper map because
it was getting hard to see the land for all the lines.
When I set the iron down my map was warm;
it smelled as if it had been left out in the sun.
I traced my fingers over familiar spots and thought
about all the places we still haven't been. As I did,
I noticed my own hands, which have folded and
unfolded this map so many times. I like my hands,
even though my skin is lined and grows thin in places—
maybe I am turning into paper! *That will be interesting,*
I thought, as I watched a blue river pulse
and go underground at my wrist.

When I was done ironing my map, I pressed a piece
of clear tape over the beginning of a hole near the Ojibwe
Marquette casino— I didn't want to take any chances
so close to home. And if you've followed me this far
it's probably time to go find your own map—
spread it out somewhere, show it a little love;
think about where you've been
and where you're going.

First Light

Near dawn my lone arm wanders
to where you laid beside me.
You always were the first to wake,
slipping out when it was still dark

after nights of glimmering, wind-laden
leaves, sleet rattling the eaves,
stars and moons, cricket tunes,
spring's long dawn chorus.

No birdsong now at the end of July,
only the gulls, far out, shrieking.
Another day of molten gold
simmers below the horizon.

I smooth the cool hollow where you slept;
I know you have already risen,
gone down to the shore
to see the first light.

Grief

I.

Here it is quiet, a mercy:
some crumbled plaster, a blank shelf.
Strips of binding from an old book
hang like parched tongues.
Nail holes leak the emptiness
behind whitewashed clapboards.
Cold light hurts. Glad
when night comes

II.

This morning a web has appeared:
where love once lived
now in every crack a spider lurks,
watching with its many eyes,
its unreason, its hunger.
I know how it waits,
                    scuttles, lurches—
I sweep the clotted nest away.

III.

By evening it is back, larger,
closer. This restless incubus throbs,
churns, pulls free,
stands. Now see how it walks,
its articulated joints; see
how its blind body whirls
with loss and desire.
From somewhere outside
I hear you calling me,
yet I cannot look away.
How can I tell you
my love is knotted into my sorrow
dancing to a music of its own
here, where only grief is alive?
See how it reaches for me,
flinging arms of fresh ink.

Waking

for Logan

Near the end of dreams, I passed
among all the strangers, touching every hand,
until I came to my own son, who'd grown from man

to child again. I knelt, his arms twined round my chest,
and mine through his— no need of words in such deep rest—
his smooth cheek upon my neck; who was blessing, who was blest?

As when I had to leave him with others long ago,
I could not fight the law he must remain. But even so,
it was enough to linger in this simple braid of grace, to know

him, who had come through me, and feel his breath
come and go. Rising from sleep, my arms outstretched,
leaving our embrace was less parting than I'd guessed.

Awake now, I wonder if, far off in his own bed
in his own sleep we somehow, lucid, met,
and though forgotten or unknown by him, yet

may his arms be light and some fluorescence pass
through him to song and string and stranger's clasp
and as for me, may dawn's gift last

for I hope now heaven may be this—
to meet in dream, the power still to bless.

Mamaangaashkaa

"...and the Spirit of God moved upon the face of the waters."
Genesis 1:2

mamaangaashkaa
mamaangaashkaa
mamadweyaashkaa
biijishimo

giizhiyaanimad
giizhiyaanimad
madweyaanimad
ombaashi

gichi-gami miinawaa gichi-manidoo
niimi'idiwag, giishkijiinidiwag
gichi-gami miinawaa gichi-manidoo,
niimi-idiwag, baapi'idiwag

baapi'idiwag

from the north and the east a powerful wind
moves over the water this day;
the eagle clings to the eyrie
and fish shelter deep in the bay

the great lake heaves in valleys and swells
as wind makes mountains of waves;
the creator and the creation
are dancing together this day

the air is filled with their roaring
in every green rise and blue trough;
everywhere white waves are cresting
as the wind and the water they laugh

they laugh

* Ojibwemowin: *there are big waves/ you can hear them/ someone comes dancing/ the wind blows loudly/ you can hear it/someone is lifted by the wind/the great lake and the great spirit/are dancing: they embrace/laughing/laughing*

(This first appeared in the spring 2019 issue of *Peninsula Poets.)*

E.M. BARRY

Not Always So

Buddha sits crossed - legged
drenched in the newly
sprouted rhubarb
contemplating the greenness
of life,
and all the erupting
possibilities.
While beneath the
forsythia, a small grey rabbit
melts into a drift of yellow
guarding it underbelly from
the neighbor's hound.

The Cabin at Burns Landing

The summer grass spreads
knee deep, broken only
by deer ambling in
silent procession to feed
on the wild mustard
growing along the trail.
In the orchard, heavy with
the scent of fallen sweetness
hornets swarm aimlessly
like half-drunk old men,
stuttering and wheeling
in the bronze tangled light.
At the edge of the swamp
the cabin waits quietly, leaning
into a brace of jack pine and birch,
tethered to earth with a snare
of brambles and wild blackberries,
it's grey logs chinked with
crumbling mud, a fringe of goldenrod
and fern knotted along its spine.
It's gaunt frame settles into
the earth, rafters open to the sun
and the nesting of swallows.
The windows pull
light from the day,
small grey bones scatter the dirt floor.
Squirrel and crow live here now
its half hinged door turns no one away.

Stopover in Union County

A mile out I hear
the thin ragged cries
drifting downward through
The yawning sky.
The sound pulls me
from the warmth,
to stand unarmed
against November's sting.
They come in low
carrying the North country
on broad feathered backs,
straining earthward to skitter
across the pond.
Great tired wings churn the water,
their weariness rises like fog
to blanket the raucous voices.
By evening cold rain, a taste of sleet;
the geese dream, long necks tucked
into pockets of down.
I pile wood on the fire,
the wind circles the cabin,
picks at windows with thin
nervous fingers.
With first light
the geese explode upward
strange black letters hurled
against the metallic sky.
Heart blood urgent now
they veer southward, their
voices strident with grief
as they rush headlong
into exile.

MILTON J. BATES

Pact

So it's agreed, then: whichever of us
goes first into the unknown country will
return and tell the other what it's like.

We have always had each other to rely on,
remember passports and boarding passes,
decipher maps and signs in foreign languages.

Whoever is first will go disembodied
and alone into the next world, unschooled
in its customs and currency, its weather

and geography. The guidebooks give few
particulars. Is it true that people there
neither marry nor are given in marriage?

Do they wake to mornings like this one,
when fallen leaves are lightly furred with frost?
When the air is crisp as bitten apple?

If you go first and return as promised
to the room where we reveled in the warmth
of goose down on winter nights; if you stand

beside our bed as though struck dumb, wavering
between presence and absence, I will know
what you can't bring yourself to tell me.

(This first appeared in *SPLASH!* [Haunted Waters Press online] in February 2020.)

Roadkill Retro-Loop

Except for a seething rice of maggots,
the twisted rag of fur and flesh lies
still beside the highway, *nature morte.*

Then the implausible happens:
ravens return and drop the eyes back in,
lustrous black and fat as plums.

The coat zips up and swells with meat.
Enamel brightens on the teeth.
The hooves glisten with wet lacquer.

A bloody ten-yard smear connects
the carcass to a car speeding in reverse,
its headlights diminishing to pinpricks.

The creature struggles to its feet,
then levers backward on hind legs,
retreating tail-first into the woods.

There it pauses to look across the road
at a moonlit trail leading to a cornfield.
The plum-eyed deer knows exactly

where it wants to go. It levers forward
on its haunches, steps onto the pavement,
and takes the impact in mid-stride.

(This first appeared in *Stirring: A Literary Collection* in December 2014.)

Missing Sisters Found Safe

April 24, 2015

The sisters were sure it was a bear.
Emerging hungry from its den in April,
it must have smelled the Girl Scout cookies
and cheese puffs. They locked the doors of their
Ford Explorer and tried to sleep.
At daybreak
on Day Thirteen, the landscape still looked nothing
like the places they called home, Nebraska
and Oklahoma. Deep woods and deeper snow,
an unplowed two-track to nowhere. But it
was all nowhere, wasn't it, in this part
of Michigan?
Thank God for their bible,
the cheese puffs, and those eight boxes of cookies.
New this year were Toffee-tastic and Rah-Rah
Raisins. Holding their breakfast ration like
communion wafers, they gave thanks, then chewed
them slowly, savoring the sugar. Maybe
next year the GSA would issue cookies
in their honor, call them—what? Leslie Lees?
Assuming they survived, Lee and Leslie
would vouch for their virtue in the field, claim
they were the peer of army MREs
and NASA food pouches, not that they had
ever tasted either.
Just then they heard
a distant roar. The bear was back, or so
they thought, until a chopper cleared the treetops.
Well, it was about time. They stepped out
to wave like those people on the TV news,
stranded on their roof when a levee failed.
Now they would have to explain how they
had missed the turn to Mackinaw City.
Which got them both to thinking: instead of
Leslie Lees, how about Mackinaw-roons?

Thaw

Hearing trickles turn into torrents,
we know the bluff behind our house
is letting go of winter, flushing it down
a dozen gullies into Lake Superior.

A neighbor's woods appears to be on life
support. Plastic tubing links his maples
to a clearing where a fire burns beneath
evaporator pans. Our lives, too, could use
support, a little sweetness after months
of bitter. Why not connect those drip lines
directly to our veins and save the firewood?

Last week my brother showed me the blisters
on his palms, all he had to show for
shoveling crushed stone onto fifty yards
of liquid clay. The frost is unimpressed
by his exertions. It keeps welling up,
turning his driveway into a truck trap.

You and I have the luxury of nowhere
in particular to go. *Thaw*, we say,
drawing out the vowel as the sun
draws vapor from the crusty remnants
of snow in our backyard. We linger
over coffee after supper, savoring
the afterglow. Your hands lie relaxed
and open on the table, as though
to gather in what's left of daylight.

(This first appeared in *Waters Deep: A Great Lakes Poetry Anthology* [Washburn, WI: Split Rock Review, 2018].)

Détente

Neither couple could remember what
word or deed had tipped the balance.
Now they detected it in every lift
of eyebrow, every compression

of lips. Without ceasing to be friends,
they had become enemies—fast enemies,
so to speak, or bitter friends. It was like
a Christmas truce observed year-round.

When they met in No Man's Land for drinks
or dinner, the men shook hands to show
they held no weapons. The talk was cordial
as before, despite a wary aspect

in the eyes, a readiness to parry
any thrust. How *triste*, they sometimes thought,
recalling the unguarded laughter
of a simpler time. There were, however,

compensations. *Love is patient*, Paul says
in First Corinthians, *love is kind.*
But can you count on it to feed the cat
when you're away? Collect the mail?

Water the plants? What bound them now was
something less than love but more than fear,
a treaty none acknowledged, yet none
could live without, least of all the cat.

(This first appeared in the Fall 2015 issue of *Peninsula Poets.*)

To a Tiny Flycatcher

You found us in the fog offshore,
trolling for lake trout, our boat
slowly unzipping the silky
surface. You arrived as though
expected, as though our party
was incomplete without you.

You troll in your own way, flying
sorties into the haze of insects
that hover just above the water.
We hold our breath when your wings
beat against the lake like a moth
at the window. Will it suck you
under this time? It never does.
You return to your roost on a rod
tip, shake out your raincoat, and bob
to the pulse of the trolling spoon.

Suppose that rod were suddenly
to register the violence
of unseen life. Would it whip you
forever from our sphere? We'll find out
if a lake trout strikes. We are blessed
for now to have you as companion
and figurehead, the visible
genius of a vast invisibility.

(This first appeared in the Summer 2020 issue of *Cloudbank*.)

A. LYNN BLUMER

Bradbury Was Right

Everyone is sizing down
to make space.
Pack your story behind a black mirror
dependent on the grid /

able to be shut off.

Blacked out of sight.

Out of Sight— the title
to the contemporary American art
horror show.

Modernism.
Our dark totems
bled in.

Empty never felt so much like home
when your hand can hold all
you've deemed necessary.

Conversations just don't carry on these artless walls /

bookless shelves.

Soon
we'll be as streamlined
as the design.

Decency

A decent home isn't existing
inside an in/
human divide simply
to compile us for
the sake of space
&the possibility of a better view.

I don't want a two
by four window to the world.

I want a shared living space
where at any chance any one
out of a multitude of challenges
could arise.

I want to find
what I fight for
as well as
something new
to surrender to.

The Huron Mountains

Bug bites
&cuts,
dug-earth trails for
wayward creatures,
dead beds of pine cushion an
outlying adventure
of rough underbrush—
Spiderwebs
&dried blood,
forty-plus mosquitos
p u l l
from each limb.
A tick, or two,
digs
in
&your brief existence is
diminutive to
these
five-hundred-year-old
trees—
billion-year-old
mountains.

Every thick inhalation
ripe with ferns
&dank detritus,
I ceded for hours dis/
connected
from the
Hectic-Human-Hive
&fed to the insects.

Go on,
take the blood,
the flesh,
&the sweat—

It's a small sacrifice.

When Swallowing a Friend

be ready
to choke.

a friend / a nutrient
you can't help
but wanna chew.

I don't like to swallow my food.

I wish I could consume less
in the world, in my lifetime.

I wish I could bathe in the flavors,
study the pallet, the history,
watch it transform
from one step to the next.

You don't always get to do that.
I didn't get to do that.

Things have to be consumed.
Everything comes to an end.

Some friends are a dish best served
to order, hot, & somewhat of a mystery
on the impact a combination just had on
your senses, that one time, in that one place.

A moment you can't recreate.

Unforgettable.

On Swallowing a Friend

He taught me
the facts really are out there,
they just take time and effort to find.

He taught me
even the middle, where the truth is often found,
is also up for interpretations.

I learned
it's just humanity.
So many variations exist, who's to say
their reality is more valued?

I learned
we will still bicker, even when
no one is getting hurt.
We bicker over the truth,

& the truth?
There's no such thing.
No absolute truth to living exists.

& the rest…
is history.

TERRI BOCKLUND

FROM A RED KAYAK

paddling into the wigwam cave at the base of the cliff
rising from Mother Superior
it smells of life reusing itself

sandstone chapel echoes trout hymns on one day
and furious prayers of thirty-foot waves the next
        cold god whose cathedral this is
        seems immoveable, unentreatable
                but look across time as the glaciers do
                and witness Creator
                turning a cliff
                into a beach

A Mercy Not Given

began with the gray she-wolf, shot
during Michigan's legal hunt
now serving unwillingly
as a hat, which means,
perhaps, that pups she suckled
and tousled in the wild rumpus den
were just so much collateral damage
which perhaps, in all likelihood,
sent her mate off into that
least-desirable status: lone;

        in which he sojourns, hunt-leader now sole hunter,
        in which, by his own unfamiliar wits, he settles for a rabbit or a rodent,
        in which his teeth never become the destiny
        of the doe with the broken front left leg
        who lives in the woods by my house,
        who is calling with every anguished step, "Here I am."

What Goes In

It’s a sin
he’d say
to leave that cereal in your bowl
when there are all those starving children.

We didn’t want it after it got
all mushy in the milk
but grandpa would swoop in
sputtering about Biafra
and slurp it all down.

Reckon there’s a sacrament
in how he ate our sins.

It’s like his famous potato sausage.
We know what goes in but it’s
a holy mystery how it all comes together.

Butch Anderson’s Potato Sausage

Makes 30 pounds

18# potatoes
12# beef
3# onions
7 handfuls of salt
¾ handful of pepper

Ivory-billed Woodpecker

Bottomland hardwood forests of the south,
old growth cypress swamps,
I hope and pray you're keeping the secrets of the
Ivory-billed woodpecker.

I bless you to be nature's failsafe, foolproof
witness protection program.
I bless you to be the reason we continue to call them
critically endangered,
to be the reason we can't quite bring ourselves to call them
extinct,
to be the cloak of invisibility they need to be
restored,
to be the cradle that rocks them to
recovery.

If I, knee-deep in your muck, breathing in your exhalations
heard the double knock, the *kent* of one calling to its mate,
spied the brilliant white of trailing wing feathers,
I'd bless myself to follow your lead,
keep the secret, knowing
the very moment it's known they are alive
they are doomed.

Campephilus Principalis (Ivory-billed Woodpecker)

I

They called you the Good God Bird, or the Good Lord Bird,
because it was the response you so often elicited.

The sight of you left us awestruck,
wingspan nearly three feet,
black feathers glinting purple, blue, then green in the sunlight,
jaunty red crest, and that bill.

That great ivory bill!

> It wasn't ivory, only the color of it.
> Perhaps this was all a terrible misunderstanding.

II

They used to say you're gone
because we destroyed your habitat.
Sure. We did that.
But we punched your ticket long before
vast tracts of bottomland hardwoods were taken
to make Singer sewing machine cabinets,
long before the cypress swamps were drained
or filled, having been determined to be
useless and offensive in their natural forms.

As it turns out, we loved you to death.

> And by we, I mean every make and model of human
> who encountered you.
> It was equal-opportunity extinction-making.

Voodoo priestesses wanted your feet,
First Nations people made clacking bracelets and amulets of your bills,
Victorian gentlemen in their fine woolen suits attached your heads to their watch fobs.

You were hunted for your feathers by collectors,
skinned whole to keep the spectacular arrangement intact.
Even Audubon himself was part of it,
shooting you so he could paint a perfect rendering of you.

They ate you, for God's sake.

They must have figured you had a special connection to the Almighty,
for they took your bones with them to their graves, clinging
to whatever power might convey them to whatever might come next.

III

Now, we gaze upon a single small feather
found in a tree cavity in Florida.
Experts peered at it under a microscope
and proclaimed it belonged to you.
Fresh, as of 1969 or so.

That inner secondary feather, encased and ensconced
at the Florida Natural History Museum
is the only proof that you survived beyond 1944.
If you did, and still do, I pray His eye is on the Ivory-billed Woodpecker
the same as it is on the sparrow.

FIONA BYRNE-RYAN

Who Are You

Who are you?
A question I never thought I would ask.
Yet, ever since we first met,
you have been pulling me closer
to hear your truth.

You lured me in. My feet became cold,
but my heart warmed, flooded with love.
Fully surrounded by clouds
my husband and I swam - those moments,
pure, like heaven on earth.

Four years later, I found my way back to you,
camped close beside your shore.
The roar of your waves whispered to my soul while I slept,
stayed constantly with me,
reminded me of your love and support.

Your name is Githce Gumi, the Great water,
Lake Superior. You visit me in my dreams.
You are my guide, my teacher.
I'm grateful to be amongst your energy daily.
As I experience your strength, you show me

who I am.

LYNN DOMINA

McCarty's Cove

If my grandfather had never left
Kiel, I would have learned
to cook apple kugel and sauerbraten
as my father liked them. I would have enjoyed
Heinrich Böll's stories without struggling
over words like *Abschied* or *gräßlichen,* though, perhaps,
every farewell would still have felt
terrible. Walking daily down crowded streets,
I might have trained
as an interpreter, learned wood carving, or worked
on the docks, loading ships with lumber,
or hand-carved clocks, or emigrants to America.

Inhaling salt air, I would have become
one of those people who misunderstands
lakes, small or great as seas, calling them insufficient.
I would never have purchased
a laminated guide, or driven
the entire tour, Superior's breadth
stretched always to my right.

This afternoon, as winter shifts finally
toward spring, I wouldn't have imagined myself,
still barely believing my luck, kneeling
in sand between the lighthouse keeper's red house
and the cove surely meant for swimming,
filling my cupped hands
with fresh water, remembering *here,*
I live here.

(This poem first appeared in *Presence.*)

No Dinosaur Ever Saw Superior

I checked out
this book, *Geology of the Lake Superior Region,*
to learn how many millions
of years ago Superior began draining into Huron
and why all that iron and copper
compressed itself into these peninsulas,
but it says, get this,
that Superior became Superior
somewhere about 7500 years ago.

What surprises me most
is that I'm not disappointed. Of course,
a lot of other things—glaciers edging north,
marine animals dying, bedrock eroding—
happened beforehand, but it's young as bodies
of water go. It'll be around a long while yet,
I think, as if that means I'll be around
a long time, too. I know
a foolish thought

when I have one. But I'm in love
with its brutal storms, its crushed ice banks,
its 3,000,000,000,000,000 gallons of frigid water,
fifteen zeroes—million, billion, trillion, quadrillion gallons,
and I love every molecule in every one of them.

The book says Paleo-Indians
witnessed ice recede, leaving
liquid water there—here—hundreds
of feet deep, though of course it wouldn't have been
like watching a wild rosebush blossom, swollen
pink buds one day, arced petals the next,
or even like a birch tree's slow release
of seed, the seed's
germination, the sapling's thickening through years.
Still, I have to say I'm jealous—
who wouldn't want to see
aquamarine bloom across a landscape
until nothing but fresh water
shirred between your footprints and the horizon,
the largest fresh water lake in the world
emerging right where you once flung
projectiles, not exactly arrows apparently
despite our penchant for calling
every marked stone we find an arrow,
but projectiles at mastodons and moose, killing
enough of them. The book
says people found drift copper
and wore it ornamentally, as I do,
but it doesn't say how much smaller
a Paleo-Indian's foot was
than my own, or if their girls
preferred warmer inland lakes,
or if, watching the lake's surface—
rough or perilous or flat—a woman's breath
ever slowed like mine.

(This poem first appeared in *The Gettysburg Review.*)

Eve Asks the Serpent for a Story

He began by telling her about rain,
how some is soft, barely mist
against her arm, how some days
her hot skin will welcome its moisture
but how other times it is fierce, frightening,
loud as peacocks or elephants, how it rushes
like owls, muddying rivers until you can't see
trout or wide-mouth bass or painted turtles.
He told her about a time
when rain never stopped, when water swirled
above the whole land.
She could have seen, if she'd been there,
ripples ring her knees, she could have felt
her waist looped by flood. Sometimes,
he said, *frightening* is another word
for *exciting.* Then he described how raindrops
linger on leaves or a grasshopper's wing or an apple's
red skin, glimmering, the apple
beautiful as ruby but still sweet, still plump with juice, still
soft on her tongue.
He was right, she knew, he was right,
as soon as she took the fruit,
bit into its ripe flesh.

(First appeared in *The Christian Century*.)

Wetlands

Riding to Boston, my friend watched
streams of rain curve
around dirt and bits of insect
on her window. She saw
hazy branches, leaves distorted by swollen drops.
Through the rain, she said the landscape
looked pointillist.

Today I walked three blocks
through wintery rain because I wanted to sit
in a gallery filled with landscapes.
The pond reflects bright clouds, and Mulligan Creek
shifts from aquamarine to brackish green.
A photograph reveals what could have been
sand dunes or an abandoned beach
if it weren't churned sludge
left by foresters. In this silence
and echoing footsteps, I am more alone
than I wanted to be.

Elsewhere, painters slump close,
their day spoiled by weather
or perhaps not entirely spoiled. Today they won't paint
here at the headwaters,
but one gazes west, committing the light, the shadow
to memory as if by her next visit
the land could be gone.

(This poem first appeared in *Zone 3*.)

Chant to Lift Up the Soul of George Floyd

Smoke hovers above the old bank building,
the shoe store clearing away
its sidewalk sale, the Indian restaurant,
the Thai restaurant, the Mexican restaurant
which yesterday served one hundred forty
orders of chicken molé. Smoke
sinks into the skinny passageway
between a new brewery and condemned diner,
beneath two floors of apartments. Smoke billows into attics,
wraps itself around photographs, scrapbooks, wedding dresses,
out through vents, out through the chink
in the wall of Harriet Jacobs' hiding place.
Smoke coats the fire escape,
every rickety step, both rusted railings,

seeps inside like haze on a tv screen
broadcasting Minneapolis set afire,
then Atlanta, L.A. We can't tell now
whether the camera films the char
of arson or the sting of tear gas. Smoke from smoldering
bricks, weight-bearing beams, red bicycle frames.
Smoke from heaps of worn tires that resist
ignition. Smoke from limbs of oak and chestnut
strong enough for a rope and the weight
it holds, smoke from the limbs
of young men. Smoke that conjures
words like *loot, riot, justifiable homicide.* Smoke from penal codes,
section 20-58, 20-59. Smoke from vats of bacon grease,
from shoelaces, from leather belts and cotton shirts.
Smoke from a lemon cake fresh from the oven,
swirling like condensation above ice cream, blanketing
chocolate kisses, Twizzlers, Skittles. Smoke from caps
stitched with an acronym, a president's
slogan, t-shirts stamped BLM
in 42-point sans serif font, smoke from initials
monogrammed on French cuffs, smoke
from Frederick Douglass' first
pair of long pants. Smoke curling
behind a reporter who shouts into his mic
into the tv. Smoke from King's royal reference,
Malcolm X's abandoned surname, smoke from names
common as Brown, unusual as Plessey. Smoke coats
a stray cat's orange fur, the veined ears of a shepherd mix,
every human being's skin, turning forearms,
the backs of hands gray, smoke stinging our throats,
filling our lungs, smoke we can't breathe,
we can't breathe, one night's or one week's residue
never enough to assuage
any man's pain, cheek scraping pavement,
a knee on a neck.

(This poem first appeared in *River Heron Review.*)

White Deer

Not the white of ice-blue glaciers
calving, nor the white of an old man's beard
flecked with gray and one or two black hairs,
nor the hazy white we attribute
to spirits, even those of us who deny
feeling haunted. Nothing
about these deer is translucent, these deer
who are not the white
of dandelion fluff, or canine or human
teeth, nor the white of little moons
anchoring your fingernails. Whiter than the white
of a cumulous cloud
reflecting noon sun,
if a cloud could be
solid, firm, a haunch moving
under its own volition. Their coats
not fur but pelt, heavy, tight, certain,
so bright they glow
as if lit
from within.
I have never seen
a white deer, just photographs
and one quiet video,
though I drive around the island,
neighborhoods where they are said to eat
rhododendrons and dogwood just like their tan
cousins, through wooded subdivisions looking,
looking. You are probably right when you say
a single vision, an ordinary animal,
its increasingly common
genetic variation, will change
nothing about my life, that a vision's
sole meaning is meaning
I've created, and you're probably right
that whatever I'm seeking already
lies within, but isn't it just possible
that a white flash leaping
over fallen oaks will illuminate
the one shadow I can't see past today?

(This poem first appeared in *Vita Poetica Journal*.)

CLAUDIA DROSEN

Parking Lot Snow Piles: Upper Michigan

—a fantasy

Farewell unbeautiful, man-shoved heaps,
darkly peppered with polluted air gunk,

Hello and welcome improved
feet-tall ice season's leavings
with not even one fleck of salt or
sand mixed in.

Gone are the singed, canned heat,
overcooked meringue peaks.
These new hills, not truck-heaved but
divinely conceived, wear baby bootie white,
are rounded, cushiony, chaste.

Chunk- and crag-free,
unclimbable, nowhere to
wedge a booted foot, these
towering piles no longer
blemish the mall terrain.

Now they are Michelin Man
mountains, soft as
Marshmallow Fluff,
with fresh folds carefully
piped out of nature's
fanciest cake tips.

Ellie Has Far-off Eyes

She's sitting on one of those high wooden stools, in the moist,
bread-baking kitchen, listening to the storm bang.

Her thumb, a pinkish raisin, lives in her mouth. It feels right in there,
comforts her when being six is tough, or just boring.

Hair smelling of the damp day, she twiddles a few matted strands
with her free fingers, inhales the scent of her mother's apron,

stiff with gluey clumps of flour,
the sweet mess of her hard work.

The room fills with the yeasty aroma of the newly baked loaves.

You. Naked.

Only the keen beam of the hundred-watt bathroom bulb
watches you lose your nightgown, scrunch it between the
towel rack and the wall, perform little rituals you wouldn't
dare declare to the office gang.

True, your resumé says you like to read, hike, bowl,
but speaking of bowl, would you let on that you
fancy reading on the bowl, shifting your weight to
get comfy, birthday suit making flatulent, cup mute
noises against the cold porcelain?

Would you share that you tend to hair that shouldn't be
there, or coax a strand of last night's roast chicken
from between your molars, flicking it into the sink?
Well, the warm, oozing truth in the cold, hard john is,
nobody's there to stare, to give a rip what you
pick, pluck or spray, squeeze, tweeze, clip or trim.

You are free to peer into the big side of the mirror,
caked with eyeliner and fingerprints, the mirror that,
like an electron scanning microscope, transforms your
blemishes into scary arthropods right out of a
fourth grade science film, maybe called

The Tick: magnified two hundred and fifty times —
a blood-sucking parasite most commonly seen-
In here, the W.C., before the game starts, costume glides on,
face gets a fresh coat of primer, it's just you. Naked.

Clearly Murder

At twilight,
an abalone
hummingbird
flickers
strobelight
wings,
buoys up,
hovers to
feed on a
sweet fuschia bud,
thwacks
Thermopane,
losing altitude,
nectar,
life.

I'm the Daughter

On the way up to my room to feed Zeke, my hamster, I'd have to pass by the living room, where my parents, Mr. and Mrs. Tragically Avant-Garde, rehearsed for a viola and piano concert at some intellectually where-it's-at place like The New School for Social Research. Mom and Dad had no office. Their daytime headquarters was the living room, where I always found them after school. I spotted Dad who blotted his forehead with a monogrammed handkerchief. He held his viola and bow in his free hand. He was not playing now. He must have had a few measures to rest while mom did her thing. Mom was standing over the Steinway. She had a butter knife in her hand. She skimmed it over the piano strings, producing an avant-garde zzzing. Mom's brows formed punctuation marks over her intense eyes.

Most other kids' moms and dads had dry cleaning businesses, or did office work. Mine played music, and if the composer called for a butter knife to be dragged across the piano strings, my folks didn't find it humorous in the least. I didn't mind. BullSHIT I didn't mind. I longed to trade them in on Ward and June Cleaver from TV's *Leave it to Beaver*, or maybe just get them a scholarship to The Normal School for Regular Moms and Dads. Bake sale moms, mini-golf dads, not entrenched in avant-garde music, written by avant-garde friends who lived in avant-garde places like "The Village."

Today, as every other day, they gave me their divided attention when they heard the front door slam. Mom's body turned towards me. *Hey, mommio,* said teenaged me, my voice still breathy from the outside. As I fled up the stairs, mom phoned in her *Hey kiddo. Bernie, can we take it again from measure fifty-two?* By this time, I was two steps away from the top, still yelling, *How goes it dad?* He echoed after me, *Oh, you know, kid. Life's a bitch, then you die. Go do your homework, ya rotten kid.* The (pardon the expression) music, continued.

These days, I'm still a short woman, no matter what the grade. Hubby and I are visiting the No-Way Cleavers in their open plan way cool house avec pool on the west coast, 3,000 from our New York roots. They're still pretty hip. They sip Nappa, and eat freakin' wildflowers. Mom is still not keyed into my life, but she and I are okay.

Dad is a different story, a book I never got to read. This trip, I look at cool daddy-o and against all the rules of cool, I grab hold of him and hug his neck. Hot tears of truth, thick as glycerin, sequestered in my ducts for way too many years, darken my father's Banana Republic shirt. *We don't hug, doll,* he's probably thinking. *At least not this way. Hugging's for backstage, after the performance, not for real, not when you're needy.*

I'm thinking we do hug. Still stuck to him like Bazooka to a 3-year-old's hair, close enough to breathe the Palmolive soap, Old Spice aftershave he still uses, these whiffs undo any last attempts to act the part of the big girl. I wail with a noise as imposing as any he and Mom have made in a concert hall. And these are not cheap tears, no. They make me hoarse, as I bathe in the release of confession. Four secret words, flung off like heavy winter weight in the warmth of the indoors: I—My hat, Love—My scarf, You— My boots, Dad—My coat.

An Amtrak Accident

I guess he must have lost his balance a bit, squeezing in hurriedly behind me in line, his luggaged arm, apparently charged with electric current, zapping me, branding a tingly patch on my back as this brand new man scented the air with his leather jacket. He said he was sorry. I wasn't. It was like fresh drinking water, his touch. I didn't know what foods he loathed, whether he played an instrument, voted a straight ticket, preferred cats over dogs, had been smacked as a kid and thought it was good for him, was too lazy to cook most nights, when he might have graduated and from where, but this accidental bump out of the cold fluorescent crowd, brought a kind of knowing that only bodies understand. The line having dispersed, he sat down next to me on the beige bench to wait for the train. I just laughed—a bit loudly at first. He looked confused, almost insulted. I told him I thought almost falling over in line was pretty funny. He laughed a little, too, and once the last echoes of giggle were over, there remained a small burst of warmth between us, at least I thought so. The kind that comes from two who now believe that one is not, after all, so very much alone.

RONNIE FERGUSON

Proper Perspective

"The Famous Tay Whale"
by William Topaz McGonagall,
a poem about a humpback whale
hunted and killed in 1883,
compelled critic Paul Godfrey
to label McGonagall
"the worst poet in the English language."
In 1958, the composer Mátyás Seiber
set the poem to music.
Seiber's score included an orchestra, a foghorn,
an espresso machine, and a narrator.
If there's any doubt in your mind,
the one who arranges an orchestra
and an espresso machine
in your honor, that's who you should marry.
You deserve it.
You deserve everything.
You're the best.

Just for You

sweatshirts are sliding
to the front of your closet
trees are starting to show
their skeletons
all the TV's in the neighborhood
stay on the weather channel
waiting for an announcement
   there's been some mistake
your neighbor stands at her window
wishing her car would start
wishing her dead poodle Sally
would scratch at the door
for a run around the yard and a piss
nightmares of the Abyss
you were warned about in church
a butterfly stuck by guts to the sidewalk
animated by the cool breeze

all these things
all these things at once
it may seem God has passed a note to Earth
you think this is bad just wait

but really
it's an illustrated love letter in flowing cursive
at the end it says
hold on
hold on i'm making all things new just for you
don't you know you've been loved
since before you were pretending to be a tadpole
in your dear mother's pond

Your Darling

she is your precious daughter
and none of the boys
asked her to the big dance

let her cry in her room
and don't make her come out
for supper

tell her she can go with girlfriends
or ask a guy friend to go
just as friends

let her change schools
and try on
different versions of herself

tell her every sad story
from when you were her age
if you think it'll help

all of these are options
but whatever you do
don't kill her

cuz you already bought the dress
and the best part of you
lives within her

and most importantly
remind her
again and again

she can choose to dance
all her life
even when she must dance alone

Your Darlings

don't kill your darlings
like some will tell you
in writing school

they are like preachers
who say you're going to Hell
if you don't stop smoking

while they choke down
one double cheeseburger
after another

with (i swear to God)
the straightest faces
you've ever seen

it's better to love
what you've found
like bird eggs without a nest

in the tender
hopeful
hands of a child

5 Truths for Today

1.
those pancakes don't need butter
chocolate chips or blueberries
they only need two things
Helen's maple syrup and your mouth

2.
naps never go out of style
neither do pajamas

3.
if you hear music   dance
sometimes you have to dance
to hear music

4.
if you hear yourself saying
i can't do such and such
as good as so and so
remember that voice isn't God
or your parents
it's not even you
it's just an old virus of a voice
passed around like a T-shirt
from thrift store to thrift store
smelly and meant for the dump

5.
even on the worst days understand
you'll still be loved
when your face is a wrinkled map
to the next life
your whole body fingerprinted
by the hot hand of time

LISA FOSMO

Looking for You, a Bear's Elegy/ A Tribute to Judith Minty

Wind breaths through trees differently here and whispers on breath,
yellow dog, grey wolf, black bear. When I last saw the bear outside my cabin,
I heard the loud clash of cymbals crashing, as the bear ran for her life with
two cubs trailing free...She was only looking for you.

The fires I kindle and tend to, the fiery breath the wood stove spits back from
the small log sauna house as I bathe with buckets and scoops. In the night air
I watch the steam escape my flesh like secret lives my bones betray as I stand
naked beneath your stars.

When I last saw the bear, he stood on haunches of back legs and peered into
my car, with eyes of copper kettles that filled with honeycombs, as I tried to leave.
He was only looking for you.

How cold bites at me or the heat of a summer night
is forgotten on the sound of wolves Howling.
I hear them barking at me like territorial dogs from the rocky ledge.
As you know nights are filled with wolves and bears.

When I last saw the bear, his massive paw prints haunting me as I often saw them
pressed into mud and sacred loam. He was only looking for you.

Hidden in minerals mined of the earth,
no more precious then breath riding the breeze on blueberry scent,
that fuels the forests lungs, on thick black fur.

When I last saw the bear he was pounding,
pounding his great paws into rock moaning thundering with all his his weight.
As if to say do not linger in my discomfort!
We said nothing to the bear, my dog and I. He was only looking for you.

Dancing the darkness at its dreams. To its very edge, and still I do not know how to speak
or even whisper in bear voice.

I know we have both touched waters that have washed over the same rocks.
I have learned the fear belongs to the bear. And when a bear dies he is just the snow
that melts away folded into riverbanks of waters that wash over our same rocks.

When I last saw the bear, he lives on in legends and poems and in your dreams ...
We were only looking for you.

Spring On Lake Michigan

I would like to say to you,
dear bringer of new,
the one holding a pinecone
in the cold early newness of spring.
There bundled in awkwardness
from the corner of the earth's room.

Though I never told you,
you are my favorite season.
My favorite smell as I breathe in
the birth of new, listen to birds arriving,
shooting like stars across the night sky
on a feathered whim.

The ice seems to be riding a floor jack,
rising till it will break.
There must be a crack somewhere,
where the rivers thaw has entered
spilling beneath the crust like a secret.
Waiting to break out onto hurried waters,
but I can see no breaks.

Only in the night I hear the war
of winter losing its battle to spring.
The sound like gunfire.
The loud thunder of ice popping.

And I'm taking sides.
I'm routing for spring.
Praying this new ruler won't turn.
Praying she won't spill waters in her hurry.

Praying she heeds her time knowing,
no one has loved her better or more.
Until winter comes again, with all the
elegance of a new bride and we will
love her all the more all over again.

But as for today, I wait for that moment.
Where once again; I will hear the roar
of rushing waters into the thaw of waves
crashing. The very sound that rattles
heaven's door.

The Fall

I can't believe how far the year has fallen.
How late the sunrise comes.
It was summer only yesterday.
Grateful for this small parcel of time.
This short passage that is mine.

The old abandoned root cellar
dug out near the edge of the woods.
An old log washed to the shore
notched for the cabin that once stood here.

This place that someone once built
How wondrous it must have been.
Now our own place overlooks it all.

The Blue Jays call out, cry like babies,
it's almost time for them to leave.
I will miss how they greet me each time.

Fly in low along the dirt road.
Their backs so impossibly blue
in the last of the evening light.

We have gathered the seasons fallen nests,
enchanted by the mastery,
the crochet of grasses, twigs,
and bark leather.
The gifts they have held
that sing us home.

When we have long gone
Who will stand in wonder of
Our timber bones.

Hummingbird Water

Spring is carried by
The return of nesting birds
Both Big and small

And what is a hummingbird ,
but air mixed with nirvana
Lite by a spark a spit of fire.

To know spring is to know forgiveness
and the return of things gone
Like the spring carnival
That comes too soon.
The air too cool.

The steel gate entrance to a ride
It's cold steel trap door
slams shut then springs open
to things that flutter and green.

There the spinning of color and warm light .
The smell of spun sugar electric alive.
Marvel at it's warm cotton candy wonder
A slice of clown hair served on a cardboard stick.

It melts the words on my tongue
I want to melt it
With rain
Make
Hummingbird water.

I long for spring
I need to say it out loud.
Walk with the words in my pocket.
Sprinkle them where things don't grow.
Feed them to hungry geese and swans
and offer them to crows and sparrows .

Sugar up all the bees
Awaken
The bumblebee queen
waiting alone in her winter cave.

An elixir,
a love potion
to welcome hummingbirds.
The air still cold
It begins to sprinkle.
If only I could melt
live as nectar.
Become hummingbird water.
All the while spinning, spinning like sugar,
on the spring carnival tilt-a whirl.

Bathing Beauties

Inside the quest bedroom at my brother's house,
my Mother lies, nestled between my sister and I.
Mom in her plush pink robe, my sister in blue satin
and me in cotton navy stripes.

Mom winces pointing her toes like a ballerina,
as her leg tightens into a charlie horse.
she kicks her leg and stretches.

We begin in solidarity throwing our legs up
in unison, higher and higher. Our arms carve air,
turning our heads in sync, as if they were adorned
in flowered rubber caps.

We are Esther Williams bathing beauties, we are
synchronized swimming, laughing unexpectedly,
with our whole bodies. Throwing our heads back
trying to catch our breath on foamy linen waves.

My father hasn't been gone a day yet.
Already we have traveled so far in the moment.
We expect grief to shatter us, to break us open,
but no one tells you about the fluidity of joy.

How it sneaks in seeps into every crack
and fissure like a salve. Soaks you to your core
poured from some unknown vessel of mercy.

No one warns you there will be joy.
And in that fresh jubilant flowing glee,
I want to whisper to my father
we haven't forgotten you.
We've only gone for a swim.

TROY GRAHAM

A Winter's Poem

Where are you humanity?
Are you somewhere between the flowers?
Are you somewhere between the trees?
Are we as humans nothing more than the show of anger,
Or some long-lasting disease?
I once saw people be kind, but now that time is gone
So keep your mask up, keep your distance
And wait for the next thing to go wrong
Or be the change, change with the day, shift with the tide
If we all learn to love again, we need not run and hide
People are fragile and often don't know what to do
If we can all learn to love again

Here I Lay

Here I lie on the floor trying to be flat as paper
And hoping that no one will see me
Everyday people walk by and don't notice me at all
And sure as hell don't want to take the time to ask what's wrong
Sometimes I just cry, I feel so alone
Sometimes I hear angry voices spitting angry words
The more words that are spoken the more I am concerned
The flowers are dying faster than they ever have before
I don't see color or race, I just see good or bad people
As they walk through the door
So here I rise from the floor now with much to say
And I'll tell you what I think
If we all don't learn how to co-exist
I believe us as humans will be washed down the sink

My Cat - Pt 2

for KD

My cat is like a stick of cotton candy, fluffy and sweet
My cat is always in the mood for something to eat
Late at night, my cat lays by my feet
My cat is not angry or judgemental and I've never heard him scream
Often times I find myself wishing my cat was a human being

GENEAN GRANGER

(1943-2019)

The Black Piano

Note appeared on the bulletin board at Daddy's work:
Free Piano – Call 863-8793

YOU HAUL

Junk to others, we welcomed it home.
An upright that smiled ith black and yellow keys,
my little brothers cheered for the stool
They spun each other around faster and
faster, and then raised and lowered
to fits of giggles or angry tears as
they'd fight over whose turn it was.

My piano delight was short lived.

Mr. Brown with his large blonde
pompadour was my piano teacher,
and playing scales and nightly
practice became my world.
Mama set a kitchen timer and
she'd listen close for pauses.
Who knew an hour could be so endless.

Mr. Brown wanted me to look professional.
To hold my fingers like a bridge with the
fingertips on the keys. To keep a penny in
place on the back of both hands.
When he wasn't looking, I'd lick the
penny so it would stick better.
Mr. Brown never caught me.
I turned eight the Christmas we
had a house fire. The piano's
smooth shellac finish puckered and
peeled like scabs. Mama repainted it
a glossy black.

Talk about an elephant in the room. O
I'd play "The Toreador Song" and my brothers'
battled war with plastic soldiers under the piano.
We got a metronome to keep time.

My brothers chose instruments on the installment plan.
Carl, an accordion and Richie, a clarinet.
Mama copied sheet music for all three of us to
save money. We joined a band called The Pip-Squeaks
with more kids. We performed on local television,
for hurt soldiers at the VA and for
ladies' luncheons. As we grew it was
harder to find time to practice, my brothers
were busy with football and baseball
and scouts. I didn't want to be seen
with the other dorky kids now that I
was in eighth grade. We canceled
lessons, didn't practice enough to
sound the way we should have.

Mama said, "No more."

The Black piano stayed silent, except
for a chorus of Chopsticks late at night.

The Mating of Loons

Praise the constancy of these black-billed birds –
their piercing cries carry over fog
before dawn breaks. Echoes from the far channel,
a distant aria, as if another wedded pair

have come to nest. They circle, dive, feed.
Each searches for the other when their
winged bodies slice the silver of the lake.

In slow concentric patterns, they waltz and talk,
flutter feathers of deepest snow and night,
wear tribal bands about their necks,
true partners in this sacred place.

After You're Gone

After you're gone, I'll forget why we bickered,
our differences, angers, complaints.
I'll remember goodnight kisses,

and early morning loving, laughter and hugs.
After you're gone,
I'll bury my face in the sleeve

of your favorite flannel shirt,
breathe in the scent that clings to the cotton.
After you're gone

I'll look for you on every street,
in each passing car. I'll search for
your walk, the back of your head.

I'll listen for your voice in each conversation.
After you're gone,
I'll hoard up stories to share,

store up caresses, remember your warmth
on cold winter nights, my body chilled
by your absence.

Over the years, when I've traveled
to far-away places, you were my home
at journey's end. After I'm gone,

in that moment between living and dying,
when we seek one human connection,
you'll be the home I'll travel to.

Pity Party

I'm gonna' tell you this world makes it
hard to be different, to go around sporting
a blue wheelchair sign. I dislike stares
that don't count me as normal. I wear a hose
in my nose 'cause my lungs really suck.

Within each a snowstorm battles, while
the body they live in weakens and wanes.
I'm more than what's not working
inside me. I pull a can of oxygen behind me
like a dead dog. Children point and whisper,

"Mama, what's wrong with that lady?" I hear
the Calliope. The Carousel's a whirl and I'm Star
of the Big Top. A us experience, I'm
a Geek in the making. It doesn't matter that I
wear lipstick, take care with my clothes.

It doesn't count that I smile and I'm pleasant,
unlike many who walk in my world. More often
than not I'm disregarded, seen but invisible,
not someone of worth. It doesn't matter that I'm
educated or that I've traveled the world. What

they see is not the *Who* that's me. People see me
lugging groceries, tipping my oxygen into a cart.
I see pity in their faces, but their pity's the last thing
I want. I'm still the *Me* that's hidden from sight.

I'm funny and smart. I've been desired, wedded
and bedded. Now, I'm seen as damaged,
less than someone who's whole.

Hello My Dolly

Nights we fell asleep to her rocking
the least of us. Mama was an orphan
never chosen. Our house bulged
like the "Old Woman Who Lived
in a Shoe." Children came to us

scarred and scared by folks whose job
it was to love them. Mama taught them
to trust again. She'd rock each one
and change the rhythm of their lives.

With a man's hanky, pinned to her apron,
she waged war on noses and drool;
wiped clean doll and baby faces. With
a string of suckers hung from a hook
she taught potty to the toughest holdouts.

Blanket-wrapped, a child, I slept
to the whir of her sewing. She fashioned
velvet dresses, fur-trimmed capes
for my dolls. Mornings she'd hold me
close and whisper *Hello Dolly.*

She found money for a bus to Biloxi
when I was 12, where a cure for asthma
dangled. Four days we traveled, me
bus-sick and Mama bent on my being
whole. I drank spoons of the elixir
until it ate a hole in the tablecloth.

Years later, when my brother was killed,
grief made her sugar climb and gangrene took
her leg. I stayed by her side. She woke
from the coma, whispered, *Hello my Dolly,*
and stayed awhile.

ALEX VARTAN GUBBINS

[Misqwaanibi] "Red River" AKA the Escanaba

I see a grey coming as I wade the weeds.
The reflection like the sky lowering itself into the water,
like the artist painted an uninterrupted darkness bank to bank.
And all I want to do is go farther down river to play the fly below the surface,
the current curling around the bedrock, the current yanking at the caddis in the eddies.
I want to listen to the deer hoof the long grasses. I want to let the rains lay out blankets
of drops onto my head as the trees soak with freshness. The wetness all around me.
The dryness of a sleeping bag a two mile walk upstream.
And only after I have lost all chances of catching a fish because I am not a fisherman,
because I do not have claws, because I cannot live on the weasel's catch,
I will turn around. I will step into the deep where the water's too clay to see,
where the white pine and the sky meet in the reflection, blurry like a Van Gogh.
The clouds shreds of nickel. The sunlight waves of birch bark. The lines I trace
straight to my heart's spirit. The quiet cave I speak of my shame in.
One of those caves on the hillsides on the way back,
where trucks travel south then north on the 581 bridge.

A Poem for the Passed: An Encomium for Aghassi Manukyan

After the service in Park Cemetery I didn't make it to,
they say your family left for California. I would've hugged Narek,

told him Gyumri's there for him, city of tuff masons,
where on a Sunday afternoon a father shows a son how to hammer a chisel

like how a father here spreads his fingers across a football and says,
        The first and third seams.

I'd have told him to catch a taxi from the statue of St. Vartan to the stone *Zdak kar*,
where to squeeze through the rock grants a wish you can wrap around a branch
        in the form of a scarf.

I'd have told him kyala's best eaten if the artist Garen shares a story
for every piece he cuts from the skull.

I'd have told him the tale of the architect who walked from Ani
        across a mountain,
eyes closed in the dark, to carry his last glimpse of an ancient church on his lids,
        lay the first corner stone to All Holy Savior's at sunrise.

I'd have told him you loved saunas because of snow and vodka,
a friend to banter with, a grill to turn lamb burgers until your hands redden
        from brushing flames and reminiscing
about Moscow when you made gold in cauldrons in your living room
        after the Soviet Union collapsed because wrestling didn't pay.

I'd have told him the first words of Armenian you taught me was
        Hayr mer, vor herkins yes,
Our Father who art in heaven.

I'd have told him when you were away from him, after you took the job in Marquette,
you spoke of him and his brothers every time we met.

Binji-Mitigwaking

Binji-mitigwaking nimikanamin mazhii'igan
indoozhigemin noodining ji-nibaa-yaang
maadaaniming gaye boonaanimang

ondweweyaaniming i'iw ziibing
ni-dazhi-ganawaabandimaanaan iniw
ni-dazhi-mbizindaanimaanaan iniw
ni-dazhi-ayaamin
diindiisi-ing gijigijigaaneshiinh-ing bine-ng
ajidamo-ng gaye waaboos-ong

Omaa ni-bi-mawadisaamin Omaa dibenjigewag Ngii-bi-izhaa ji-bizindawangidwaa.
Gishpin gaawin inoondawaasii nagamod ingotaaj gii-bi-izha bakaded zhigos gaye obiinaan
maji-manido-wan
Gishpin gaawin inoondawaasii nagamod ingotaaj gii-bidaashi makade-aanakwad-manido
gaye obiinaan aakoziwin

Bineshiinh owaawanonan ingotaaj bii-gosegnig
Waawan-Wigwanan bibagaanan indego Ogaa-oninjiganan
In-ga-dinitam-min iniw na, maada'amaazonid banajaaniwan
Da-daanginan-an oshkaki-mikwe o-zidan-iwan na
Da-Baashkaabigwanii-n ashkibagoon na, ezhi-mino-w-anaa-mo-yaang

(Translation)

Inside the Forest

Inside the forest, we find a cut-over clearing.
We build camp at the place of the wind so we can sleep,
at the place where the wind picks up and where the wind dies down,
at the place from where the wind blows from a certain place of the river
at the place we watch those others
at the place we listen to those others.
We exist at the place of the blue jay, the chickadee, the grouse,
at the place of the squirrel and the hare.

Here, we are visiting. Here is their place. We came to listen to them.
If I cannot hear singing, I am afraid the weasel has come hungry and brought the *manido*.
If I cannot hear singing, I am afraid the black-cloud spirit blew in and brought a sickness.

I am afraid that the other eggs have broken.
Shells are thin like the fin of a walleye.
Will we hear these others, those little birds singing?
Will the new-earth-woman touch their feet?
Will there be new leaves so we can breathe?

JOHN GUBBINS

WATERS:

The Bering Sea at Norton Sound

On the Bering Sea one's portion is risk. Ever determined and patient, the Bering is a constant threat. On windy days, waves born off Kamchatka chug onto Alaska's west coast, pulverize shingled strands, and swamp boats. The Bering spends little time with wreck victims, numbing their arms and legs before invading their body core to suspend their hearts. During winter, it works quickly, killing its victims in fifteen minutes. During summer it lingers over killing them, sometimes taking an hour. All go numb stroking for shore. Euphoria sets in. And shortly they succumb, food for crab, and smiling at the prospect.

Oblivious to human aspiration, the Bering fosters puritan purpose. No sunbathers lay out on blankets along its shores. No tourists wade its shallows. No discarded tubes of sun screen litter its beaches. Kayaks, skiffs and ships alike risk it only when they must. To attend relatives, to collect berries and shorebird eggs, to put hunters on seal and walrus, to put fishermen on crab, salmon and herring. And nothing else.

Young fisherman risk the Bering for one reason. For them Alaska is not the last frontier nor is it a land of opportunity. For them Alaska is the place where the sea puts you on trial for your life. They revel in the gamble. Year after year they work the Bering wagering their lives, a poor man's wager, and take on heaven and earth, wrestling with the gods of the winds and the waters. They yearn for that brief moment when death stands before them, and by dint of will, they vanquish it, so becoming a lord of the swells…a lord of the deep

To most observers the typical fisherman is a profligate, often blowing months of wages in a week ashore. And it is true many fishermen pay little attention to the practical. Money is not the prize. The prize is triumphing over the worst the Bering can hurl at them. The practical have their bank accounts. Fishermen have their sagas. Sagas live forever.

Today our heroes come from the most unreliable among us, from wanderers like Bering Sea fishermen. Looking for redemption, they will commit all they are and have with no consideration of the morrow. Thus freed from their future, they can accomplish what the reliable judge impossible. And perform the heroic.

The Nushagak River at Dillingham, Alaska

Bristol Bay spread out before me as a freezing drizzle began to fall. Unlike pictures of touristy Alaskan scenes, Bristol Bay shows no rocky cliffs, no rugged head lands, no dripping glaciers. Instead it displays an utterly flat scape, the level prospect of the Bering Sea to the south and west and barely elevated above it a few landmarks setting off the remaining compass points. To the northeast, close at hand, lay Clark"s Point with its sand dunes. To the west lay stretches of brown tundra relieved by scattered spruce trees and the black volcanic cones of the million and a half acre Wood-Tikchick State Park. To the north, the last compass point, lay the Nushagak River, its Estuary, and the town of Dillingham.

The Nushagak drew my attention. Annoyed by its plunge down the Nushagak Hills, the river skirted Dillingham preferring to slow and wallow in the shallow silt flats beyond, the stuttering entrance to its estuary. There is no sure footing here. And no cheer. Salt marshes, scourged daily by punishing tides, decorate the river's shifting banks with drear tufts of cord grass. Listlessly, the river bows, respectful of their meager efforts, and moves on, for its true interest lies a few miles farther on, Bristol Bay, the watery caldera where the sea and all the great salmon rivers of Western Alaska consort. Only there, finding community, does the Nushagak halt and begin its dialogue with the deep.

Soft spoken, the river opens the exchange conversing clay and silt. And as a polite host might take a guest's coat, Bristol Bay relieves the river of its grimy burden closeting it until the next turn in the tides. Punctually, hours later, the sea flood returns, collecting the river's off scourings and sifting them like drifting ash back onto the estuary flats. Anchor chains jangle and boats slam against marina piers in the foamy rush. Delivery confirmed. The estuary quiets, the river inert in the face of the flood. Hours pass and then, just as predictably, the sea flood relaxes releasing the paralyzed river to speak once again. And the monotonous ancient exchange starts all over, a recurring argument between two physicists pressing each other with the precise mathematics of river gradient and the incidence of the tides.

The Mississippi River

Busing from Seattle, I fell asleep, waking in Minneapolis. East of downtown, I94 crosses the Mississippi River, just below St. Anthony Falls, I strained in my seat for a glimpse downriver where the Mississippi flowed, darkly reflective, waiting to color in the dawn. My mind mapped out an imaginary canoe trip. With eight days of hard paddling, I imagined I could make Wyalusing where the Wisconsin River joined the Mississippi. And from there it would another two days up the Wisconsin to our house. Every hour I ever spent on the river came back to me as I charted my course.

There were the evenings alone on islands swept clean by flood and wind. The river sounds engulf you, herons and cranes croaking to their rookeries, the scream of bobcat and raccoon, the wail of coyotes, and the repetitive calls of frogs and crickets. Set against this din you hear the splashing of great fish chasing down prey. You see their swirls and calculate their size, five and six feet, maybe more. Blue cats, gar, sturgeon, pike, and so many others, robust specimens thriving in this living museum of every species that ever swam this river.

Your campfire is the only light. It burns to coals and the real dark descends. And you fall asleep because somewhere in that deepest part of yourself, you remember the night sounds as you remember breathing. You dream of belonging, of belonging to this island, its sand and muck, and to the river which inundates it each spring washing it clean of all human sign, a blank slate on which to write the meaning of your life.

The blare of a tug horn wakes you in the morning. Late summer, morning mists hang low over the river. Thick, they chill you and hide side channels and shorelines. Morning tea and the rising sun drive them off, but not before banks of fog swallow up the dawn and glow pink like thunderclouds shot through with lightning. The sun climbs higher, the mists depart leaving dew, the freshness sprinkled by dawn's aspergillum, a holy blessing on all who wake by a river.

Below LaCrosse, three and four miles wide, the river reminds you of your insignificance. Your canoe becomes a fluttering leaf bouncing on the river's currents. Out from shore, in full daylight, alone, the canoe's gunwales sit a mere foot above the sheet of charging water, a mobile world, like the back of a swimming turtle as told in native origin legends. Your eyes search left and right for the shoreline, for context, for the familiar, and see only moving water alongside keeping pace with your strokes. Finally surrendering any hope of context, you fix your attention downriver. The whole world slides towards New Orleans. Hour after hour this perception overwhelms you, and your eyes grudgingly adopt the watery film of the river's flow. All else, birds, islands and boats are double exposed on your retina. A shake of the head, a lowered hat brim, and you grow blind to all but the next fifteen feet of the river ahead. Stroke. Stroke. Stroke. Threading carefully through stump fields and pointing the canoe's prow again and again into the wash of river barges. Hard paddling. Before long, it is twilight. The river mists begin to build. A clean island ahead. Drift wood for fuel. Tea, bratwurst and a few potatoes pulled from the fire. It was a good day. You are going home.

The last town before Wyalusing is Prairie du Chien, the oldest town on the river north of St. Louis. For three hundred years the whole of the Northwoods met here every spring to barter. These days after the spring floods subside, children hunt for arrowheads and axeheads among the debris the floods unearth. They keep the best. As I sit here now, I turn over in my hand, intact, delicate bird points, hundreds of years old, found in the meadows of Prairie du Chien, the work of sensitive, skilled artists, their names forgotten. Hundreds of years from now no one will touch anything so beautiful left by me.

Below Prairie du Chien the Wisconsin River enters the Mississippi. It would be a two day paddle from its mouth to Muscoda and our home. Towering above the river stands Wyalusing with its sheer five hundred foot limestone cliffs. Peregrine falcon nest its heights. At its base a rock walled canyon concentrates the Wisconsin's powerful currents to whitewater, the only rapids on the lower river. No canoe can breast its waters, So my trip ends. Stranded. No more rivers between me and Madison, I sit, in reverie, empty.

KATHLEEN M. HEIDEMAN

Miracle in the Museum of Iron Industry

About suffering they were never wrong
- W. H. Auden, *Musee des Beaux Arts*

About rusting they were never wrong,
our deep-shaft miners: how well they knew
the holy mystery of oxidization; how it must take place
in the permanent exhibition's swarm of long-beaked pick-axes
preserved like feeding mosquitoes, rust corroding each iron proboscis
(only the Curator doesn't know) where it pierces the faux-rock wall;
or the crowbar rusting in the mannequin's tireless grip, prying
more imaginary ore from the roof of the humid, recreated drift
— how, even as our own devout mothers idle in the stormy
confessional of the Brushless-Touchless Car Wash
as the rocker-washer regathers its dripping bowels for a final
underbody pass of Rust Inhibitor — how even then
there must always be a boy reinventing the wheel, a girl feeding
nails to a chirping nest of open-mouthed jars, each crucible
translucent, half-filled with kerosene, vinegar, Diet Pepsi,
Palmolive, milk, urine — *"she'll never lose her love for cooking, that girl"*
but few will understand her search for God: *Rust,* the Secret Recipe by which
one substance alchemically becomes another, that dreadful Rorschach
she saw once, in *A Child's Big Book of Bible Stories, Illustrated* —
the Stranger's secret identity revealed by his hands, palms up: red holes
eternally unhealed. For every father buying *Rustoleum,*
for every martyr with his finger in the dam,
there's a girl like her, with her pocketknife in the family's rusting fender,
widening the wound — *for Curiosity? for chrisssake!*

Catching iron flakes in the cup of her upraised palm.
Even in Brueghel's painting of Icarus: how well we ignored the Descent itself,
as if the child would merely drop into an entry-level position in the mines.
Beneath the flaking pigment, x-rays of Icarus reveal an earlier failure:
Still Life with Hard Hat, some fatally-dented relic from the fall.
Otherwise, the paintings are the same: undulating sea, umber field,
the distant oredocks, the gaunt, omniscient eagle with a fishhook rusting in its beak.
We swore we heard the distant rumble of failure, or was it the armbones
of an angel flapping as the final feather loosened...?
None of your damn business! the mine foreman warned the guy who pointed,
so we kept our eyes averted, and rot — because we failed to stop
when the first shoe dropped — rot found a nailhole in the hoof,
a weak spot in the tunnel roof. My god is dark, thought Rilke.
The clouds dropped. Then the horse fell lame; it thundered hard.
Whatever we were ignoring grew larger, approaching. Like a raindrop.
(This poem was first published online in *Queen Vic Knives* (defunct).)

Evidence of Deep Negaunee

Let us mosey, you and I,
where moneyrock's been piled against the sky
like an injured miner immobilized on a stretcher —
let us limp through miles of half-subsided streets
to the puttering retreat of beers at Eino's tarpaper camp
or Toivo's barroom floor strewn with peanut-shells
the former streets heaved by frost
leading us to a dead-end fence —
O, do not say "Rusty, what da' hell's gotten in you?"
Let's crawl beneath the barbed-wire and continue!

🠻
It's against the law to be in here
but in the distance you make out the shape of others:
an elderly couple holding hands, him helping her
step over the half-downed fence, *terra tremula,*
cratered as after a long bombardment.
There was a town here, our Location;
it wasn't always off-limits, like a lover's heart it was
partially known, surface-mapped, core sampled.
We cut the land into lots and marked it
with metal stakes, their tips painted cherry-red.

🠻
The owl — she hunts the shore of Lake Superior
for elusive words, crayfish between cobbles,
among Negaunee gravestones she hunts mine rats —
O look! it "hoots and swoops
and catches a mouse"[1]
by *Beloved Wife* and perches, tearing flesh, upon *Paavo's* marker —
something further here,
red-whorled sandstone already rain-eroding, the owl devouring
and relieving itself — *Husband Lost to Cave-In, Sorely Missed &*
Sorely Recalled

---

[1] a quote from Dylan Thomas, *Under Milkwood*

🠗
I sing of Rusty, strong-dumb-true
he milked the earth of iron for you
and harbor-baled the fish you ate
and hated those you said to hate
and mined the fields for tenderloin
and shot down eagles for your coin

🠗
Come Sunday, closing hour,
we'll come wheeling out of Cuchuli's Bar and stare
bleary-eyed across the highway to the railyard
where we worked all day loading logs, sap perfumed
and stripped to our waists in sunlight, ankle deep
in mud, remembering places we fell face-down,
running, or skinned the bark from knees
while Cuchuli's jukebox chases us into the night
with Sheryl Crow — *when you gonna learn?*
You're just an empty cage girl if you kill the bird.

🠗
Whose gate this is? I guess I know.
The road is posted "Private"
though his real home's
far away from here. Downstate. He's rich,
I hear. His buddies come to shoot 'his deer'
and buy our girls some beers
and knock them up, and talk us down
and drive golden SUVs through town.
His cabin's fancy, wooded, deep,
and I've got promises to keep.
And I've got matches and kerosene.
And I think you know what I mean.

🠗
An iron dust presses her red lips against Empire's windowpane
and blows us a kiss, an iron dust rubs her ruddy rag
against the pane, as if to caress —

🠗
Come Sunday, millennia hence,
our descendants may worship
beneath the vast stone roof of Stope #2
where the simplest prayers
echo and rebound, re-doubling, swelling

exponentially, prayers to a deity
from whose shimmering Womb so much was blasted
— gnostic hardrock from which our fathers' hallowed
half-remembered-names hollowed out a Great Stope,
a holy room. So we'd descend to awe. So we'd kneel, too.

🠻
Come Sunday,
if such a worshipful word may be uttered in times like these,
we'll go down to Park and Cherry, help our neighbors
pry Immanuel Lutheran off her foundation
and drag it brick-by-heart-broke-brick
to solid ground —

🠻
O Mineral Creek, Pyrites Road, Iron Street!
Of thee we strolled & sing & failed to sing
& now are sore afraid —
we blinked, we feared the dark
& now walk backwards into the remembering
eleven year old boys led mules, *hey mister!*
sixteen year olds worked drills
hernia'd men braced up widow-makers
between floor and ceiling
& watched over their shoulders
for something coming, some hurt gust,
dreamt rock-burst, gut instinct…

🠻
Our father Iron Mountain
pine-tree'd hollowed mine
thy caved-in domes, thy work in earth
done as in heaven —*iron*
giving our men their daily ore
their chores, forgiving our trespasses
& more. You trench into us now
grave undermining against us
yet bury us not in thy stone heart
& deliver us again unto surface.

🠻
Rusty'd pocket a bottle of baby oil
and him and me, we'd spend all day on Cedar Beach.
Rusty was lifeguard that summer, kept saying
I could save your life; bragger, he never did.

Save my life? I swam like an otter, rolled and dove,
didn't need him. But something in my gut fluttered fins
at the sight of him. Rusty, midsummer, was berry-brown
— all but a spot like a thumbprint, where the whistle
dangled from a string around his neck, pale tattoo.
That was the last summer I loved everything:
big-mouthed boys on sun-warmed towels,
the way my long hair dried in snakes around my head
coiled to strike, the green smell of water, *Rusty.*
My good ear against the earth, I heard the future —
the distant scrape and shudder of Empire,
machinery coming all summer, booming,
long before the water levels started dropping,
before I knew anything about anything, really,
I knew they were chewing at *what I knew,*
digging a money-hole like there was no tomorrow
— a pit ballooning like Rusty's sister Helen pregnant
by that dumbass who drove head-on into a dump truck
fully loaded, Empire giant. My father swore they could'a buried him
in a manila envelope, stone cold sober, no swerve, knew what he was doing.
At the bottom of Empire
my uncle ran a machine with a yellow jaw, gnawing, filling;
my father manned the pellet plant kiln, hot as hell.
That Hole puts food on the damn table, he said,
but Rusty and me, we lived on sunlight
that last summer he was thin and brown,
and I believed —

🠋
How do we keep drilling into unmapped adjacent stopes, emptied & inundated?
How'd that kid tumble into a shaft which never, according to our maps, existed?

🠋
Come Sunday, Rusty turns from the surface world.
I un-marry you, he tells the woman asleep in his bed,
I quit, he tells his flask, his company hat, his cigarettes,
the yellow excavation bulldozer ready to purr against his leg.
Rusty stomps away through subsiding meadow,
rolls under a rusting fence
saying: *hold on dark-haired girl, I'm coming, I'm* —
Sleepwalking. Clambering over rubble,
falling to his knees at a ragged shaft-hole
hidden in grass, glint of broken-mirror sky
far below, a glimmer of precipitous drop.

🠻

There's been an artist around town, the *real thing*
with a canvas bag full of paints and brushes, easel
in a sling across her back.
Someone saw her painting from a vantage point
atop Jasper Knob, another saw her
on the Bancroft shoreline, sketching how the
twin headframes dominate our scene,
cement sphinxes flanked by iron hills.
Rusty said he stopped to watch her working —
What can I say? No rocky shoreline,
no lake, no pines, no dramatic skies,
no steeples, nothing!
Only wild smears & squirmings,
green shark-toothed scribbles,
a boozy maelstrom of colors mixed
as by a funnel cloud, and where our town should have stood,
our old mines, our named things recognizable and good?
She'd seen only flooding, clawmarks, ooze.

🠻

The mine quit dewatering
thirty years ago, he tells tourists.
Turned off the lights and the Cornish Pump,
water's just below this cap now, he says,
tapping his boot against cement. Smears of specularite
mark the tunnel walls connecting *Dry*
and *Shaft.*
You can call me Virgil, says Rusty.
His stained skin's a map of local ores, porous tunnels
where he wormed his way below our streets.

🠻

Come Sunday, he recalls, she fills with water
& we pump her out, five hundred gallons a minute
but it pours back in, the water runs home
like that burlap sack of kittens my dad dumped in the Dead River —
he always claimed they found their way back to our porch
by week's end. Same kittens, but different.
Mewling for milk & howling for meat.

🠗

Come Sunday, he'll glance down at his wife's hand-mirror
and for a moment his glance falls bottomless,
eye to eye with himself, a lower half he doesn't know about yet,
some maze inside Rusty he hasn't mapped.

🠗

Rusty strolls in dripping from the shower,
says let's get dressed up, babe, go to church down in Iron Town
just for the hell of it — let's take communion on our tongues
and take the wafer out again, and look at it under a magnifying glass,
let's get upset, and whisper, and storm out. Let's dissect it,
act like something's missing, something critical, and it's our job
to find it. Let's act like we can't agree what the Clues mean,
let's pretend we're detectives fighting over a Mystery!

🠗

Elsewhere, the giant drill bit being used to rescue stranded miners breaks. Progress halts, halfway. A deep rescue hole must be drilled, can't be drilled here, must be drilled in a new spot. The search for a new drill bit begins while the governor says: I spoke with the families — these are mining families. They're tough, hopeful people. Prayerful people. The miners go: tap, tap, tap. To let us know.

Areas of Induced Subsidence

> The Mine Inspector provides yearly programs at schools (...) regarding the dangers of open pits, shafts and fenced caving areas. Stickers for distribution to students have been printed that read "Caving Grounds are Not Playgrounds"
> - Marquette County Hazard Mitigation Plan, *Chapter 5: Unstable Ground.*

If her body isn't, after all, where he pointed,
where'd her body go? We all know
he off'd her. Deeper, maybe. The mine pit.
Unimaginable murk there. Twisted equipment
corroding into horrible dragons, they'll find her
caught in one of the bucket's talons, they'll pump
or drag bottom come spring. Or Dead River maybe,
where Doc Mudge threw a burlap bag of pups to drown?
Only it didn't work. There was a hole.

Subsidence comes often in the saturated spring,
the ferrous earth opens like a sponge, holding meltwater
while light hovers later each evening
and the sun practices holding its breath.
Birds wade into the reddish muck of Orey Creek
on long legs, dip their heads below the icy surface:
just checking on things.

It never works, the squirming burlap bag. There's that hole,
a rip in the unthinkable, a seam through which we swim away
mewing, barking, wagging our tails, ready to forgive anything.

Neighbors reported deep rumblings,
Was it possible that an old cap had fallen at the Frances Mine?
No visible evidence on the surface. Periodic re-inspections will occur.
At midnight, an old board yields to rot
and drops, a small throat opens under grass,
an unmarked shaft parts the grass with parched lips.
The dog goes to investigate the hole
and it swallows: barking, compost pile,
stacked terracotta pots, patio slab.
Nobody sees nothing. Nobody hears.
Near dawn, a puff of fog drifts from the lawn's little nostril.
One of the old gods, remembering how to breathe.

⬇
By which names do we praise the pondweed, the pine,
the mosquitoes? In Babylonia it was said *there were too many gods*
– we remember the names of only a thousand now.
Their gods loved like humans, and could die.
And what happened, if they died? They found
an underworld deeper than our own — down, *down!*
Are we there yet, walking among failed deities,
inching our way deeper than grief?

⬇
The physicist Seaborg was a god born of our Iron Range but later
probing intimacies of the atom down to such-&-such valence
and the naked nuclei's subatomic qubit,
wished to tell us how we came to be here, describing
within micro-fractions of a second *what happened after Bang*

⬇
For the brain's inner corrugations may change w/cataclysm, just as the mine's dynamiting changes the terrain & as for myself, fresh-shattered, bent to palm a hand of dust, red ore soft between my fingers. I let it run to form a cinder cone, a barren heap. I named it *Rusty,* claimed it as my new home.

⬇
Rusty was a nervous kid, asking about the cave-in zones, *but why?* & Rusty's grandpa grabbed him by the collar, shook him hard, said you listen good, we were paid by the ton for what we hauled up, they didn't pay for safety, for time spent timbering, there was no hourly wage, there was only ore — we set them timbers as far apart and as fast as we could, and we got to work. That sinkhole will put a shit like you through college.

⬇
Doesn't the worm know each square foot
of this town, *by taste,* by heart?

⬇
Later our mines grew entangled underneath,
several shafts serving a merged orebody,
all hollow stopes, a heap of jack-o-lanterns
piled in the garden, frozen mouth-to-mouth,
their features collapsing, warm winter days,
until a grin was a gasp. Even our rats,
said Rusty, wore hard-hats.

⬇

The box promises "Kills in one feeding" but if you believe the label, she says,
I'll show you their holes. *They're a different breed, mine rats,*
monstrous big. Rig a camera to detect motion
and you'd see how they burble nightly to the surface like a fountain,
rats like rusty water pouring from a pipe.

⬇

On the flank of the Chapin subsidence I found Rusty picking wild strawberries in the ditch, snipping each red heart from its earthy stem with a thumbnail, gently transferring that sweetness, palm to palm and rolling 'em into a Pump-&-Go mug.

⬇

Someday, sweetheart, Rusty swears, *the Great Stope will collapse.*

⬇

By candle, by flickering, by the glow of carbides pinned as boutonnières to our helmets, we cast shadows, underground. They greeted us by name, friendly Shadows, they clapped us on the back and sat with us unseen as we warmed lunches on a shovel, drilled holes, ran fuses. The price of a candle or carbide was deducted from each man's pay; every wick, every matchstick was counted. As our eyes grew accustomed to the dark the work we did there got ever more shadowy, *aren't we right now 'bout under your basement, Toivo?* a cousin jack called down-stope and we'd howl with laughter. We drilled our holes under schools and cemeteries and mucked them out with a shrug. Our Shadows drilled shadow-holes, set shadow charges, stood indifferent as our drifts exploded in eruptions, as roofs caved or red dust reduced us to coughing fits, blasting smoke, a taste of dry blood. Men bought their own blasting powder, caps, and fuses; it is undeniable to say they skimped on certain "safety standards" in order to meet quota, in order to blast and finish mucking before the whistle. Clocks ticked on without concern for conditions; so many costs deducted from a miner's earnings it was said that *everybody's grandfather paid the mines for the privilege of mining* —

⬇

It happened in those days, then, that our Shadows started following us up-shaft at night; pulled us into local bars for a beer'n-a-bump, kissed our wives, hauled our garbage to the dump, left long hematite smears upon our sheets in the shapes of men. Shadows never bled, were never blown up or crushed under collapsing backs, pinned by orecars or pummeled by rock. We blasted harder in the war years, inkier, everything was Shadow. It got to the point you couldn't tell, running into a man after shift, if it was him or his Shadow except maybe the eyes, if they were brown or green or only darkness.

⬇

Shadows profited. Shadows ate well and grew bellies that got in their way as we pounded and shoveled; they leaned back and took it easy. Then Geno Beltrame electrified the first mine — *Let there be Light! Bare wires and naked bulbs!* and our Shadows skedaddled, cowered, puddling underfoot, quit climbing ladders, quit slipping in the mancar with the rest of us. For a while, it seemed we'd rid ourselves of our Shadows. *Got our wives back!* some joked, but others worried. Weren't they down there lonely, still waiting for us? Weren't they sleeping on our behalf in seeping seams of hematite, in groaning rock, in terrible damp stalls where each mine formerly kept blind ponies? In short, they were abandoned, and bitter.

🠗
And thus we grew to fear our Shadows.

🠗
One day on our lunch break,
sitting in the great stope where rock-bolted walls
rose on either side Rusty hollered "An earthworm!
How'd it get down here?"
It squirmed on his shovel, illuminated like a Caravaggio
& we beamed our head-lamps down, agape.
Then we all leaned back. Looked up. Beamed our lights
at the ceiling, a hundred feet above our heads,
each of us fearing we'd glimpse some flicker of sunlight
the sharp tip of the wife's garden trowel piercing —
pinholes of noon-light. *An omen!*
muttered Toivo and all shuddered.
But good or bad? said old Mudge.
What da hell! said Muck.
But Rusty, our brave boy, he slid that worm into his lunchpail
and returned it to the surface after work
like he was trying to reverse some curse.

Getting the Visions

> After this oracle
> there will be no more oracles…
> The precinct is hereby desanctified.
> - Alan Dugan, *Last Statement for a Last Oracle*

Our kids gather in the Dolomite quarry to huff rusty gas-tanks, or worse, metal spray paint swiped from the hardware store, sprayed into paper bags. They press the bags to their lips, inhale the vapors and their eyes roll back in their skulls — our kids, damn it! When a priestess at the oracle was suspended over a volcanic gas-seep until she spoke gibberish, everybody called it prophecy. *Deep Negaunee,* the social workers call it. We've fallen deeper than we fathom. Oh, they try to deny it, our kids swaying home with dilated eyes, denials seeping from silvered nostrils and gold-leafed lips, too high to check themselves in a mirror. They call it *getting the visions* — Eino's own sweet little girl Rosa got into it hard, huffing god-knows-what from rusty tanks down in a mine pit at the old Athens, now she wanders Iron Street like a half-wit prophet, telling us to make a sacrifice, calling men *The Monsters.*

Eino tried to get her treatment and how does she repay him? Rosa shows a counselor at Bell those tattoos she can't explain, says there's someone living under her bedroom, a wild man who comes to her bed at night, snorting and pawing open the floor with his red muddy boots. Protection for Vulnerable Adults folks, they called on poor Eino — can you believe it, like he's grown horns in his old age, molesting his own motherless girl? *Nobody's living downstairs,* he told them, *hell, there's no basement under my home. This house is build on solid rock —*

Solid rock! Eino repeated, down at J.D.'s Shaft, retelling his outraged story for the umpteenth time. Solid rock, you say? — we tease each other like a pack of yellow dogs — solid rock, eh! You worked a mine beneath that very street yourself, you old horny liar. Maybe set a meat-trap for the minotaur, maybe wire yourself to the bed, maybe check Rosa's floor for a trapdoor, like in that fairy tale about dancing princesses. Ah, you know what I'm meaning, scowls Eino, she ain't climbing down no mine ladders at night — she's hit rock bottom boys. It ain't funny and we know it, so we quit joking. Rosamunda, poor girl, she's lost in the head-maze now, passing back and forth through solid rock like drifting vapor and Eino says he don't know how we'll ever get her back.

After Iron's Boom Goes Bust

No industry in this port town's future, only tourism
based on a memory of industry, and relics for sale
including postcards no one sends, craft beers named
for mines, smoked fish, pine slivers, iron pellets in baggies.
I captain the oreboat, Paavo B. Tiresias, paid to stay
just out of sight, anchored nightly behind the island
— not a bad job. Appreciative crowds gather
on the breakwall with their cameras. Down at the oredocks,
taconite spouts slip into place with grease and wires,
a rehearsed ease. The rumbling of the ore as it enters
is pre-recorded audio. Red dust lifting in the wind billows
fresh from the deck where we've sprinkled it, each morning.
After iron's boom goes bust we extract Scenery & Trust.
Bilge and ballast automatically adjust to make the
freighter ride lower, leaving harbor. Faux smoke seems.
A cardboard crew. A tugboat just for show, helpful.
Departing, I sound the ship's foghorn — kids love it.

JOHN HILDEN

Insupportable

You weren't there when it hit
On your return to the bridge
your pole is gone...
Sheer chance you see
something metallic
glinting in the water
You fish it out with a stick
unaware you've hooked
a bottomfeeder
You see a flash of scales
as it surfaces in the murk
An illusion drops away
as your monofilament snaps
You stumble home giddy with relief

Elegy For a Friend

You've already been gone
for a number of years
as I pass a guy in
the foyer of a hospital
failing to recognize him
as your roomie from
our college days
As recognition dawns
I wonder if his thoughts
on the manner of
your death chime with mine
bold face to our lower case
your Harley colliding with a bear

English Teacher

No one believes you
when you say you saw
an island of sanity
in the eye of a blackbird
The bird is perched
on a post as you pass
a driver pulling out
shearing off
your front end
The ambulance crew
writes it off as shock
as you chase down
student papers in the snow
speak of an incandescent shore

Don't Delve Too Deeply

Others don't mind walking past
that spot in the creek
where the undertaker's son
drowned a bag of kittens
You give a wide berth
There are reasons for this
but sometimes it is best
to take your own advice
as you wake from a dream
in the middle of the night
haunted by a cloaked figure
with a club raining down
destruction on the heads of frogs

Crisis At 4 A.M.

If I could slip past the sentry
of my conscious mind
I might get back to
what passed between
my cousin Chuck and I
as we met on the grass
where Vern's store
burned to the ground
Today I saw a zealot
on a downtown street
a man who'd flown
too close to the flame
He tried to catch my eye
but I cut him dead
I sense a steep incline ahead
abandoned heights I must regain

TARA CHANNTELLE HILL

Pirate Heart

He told her if she quit smoking,
he'd do it every day. He'd do that for her.
He couldn't kiss a girl that smoked,
but he could leave her in oleander
to rust and clay. It's easy to say words like Yoga
when you live in LA. And it's easy to drift
in clouds of carcinogens and shots of Stoli
under flaccid skies of unyielding gray.
He liked where she was. Fingers bent
towards the past told her to run. Run.
Run. She was taking out the garbage
and saw him reading his novel up in a spaceship
over Negaunee. He didn't look as distant
as the night he left her. And he didn't like
confrontation so she performed a sun salutation
then flicked her cigarette at him to say goodbye.
She'll take her next steps in silence,
with children and jam jars full of wine,
for another man who likes cheap grape cigars
and never forgot where home was.

(First published by Virgogray Press.)

For Dorothy

A salmon colored petunia reaches for the sun, alone and separate from the rest in the crack of my grandmother's front porch steps, it looks like she's blushing. She, my Grandmother, quieted, rocks on her porch swing. Before Alzheimers stole something from us, Dorothy would be much more chatty on mid-summer evenings. I remember louder times, how she used to play poker with her friends at the Marquette Golf & Country Club - after they played the back nine - with their bras streaming from their clubs on the back of her gas powered golf cart. Pennants waving to the lifelong anthem of a Lake Superior blue-eyed courageous woman. A woman who talked back. A woman who refused to go back to the Catholic church because someone there called my half-black cousin a nigger. "They're God-damned hypocrites," she warned, often.

Now, time is bent.

Now, I care for her like she did for me when I was a child. I hold her hands. I put cocoa butter lotion on her tired skin. Her limbs and armor, speckled and sun-spotted like an inland trout. We try to sing along to the once familiar tunes of 'Saturday Nights with Elmer Aho' on the radio, but her mouth seems hooked. I try to tell myself time is not so linear when a warm South wind blows and sweeps her long white hair across our faces and taps my round belly. I wish my unborn baby could meet the old her. I wish she could scold me like she used to when I'd peel the birch bark off the trees in her yard. I wish when I looked into her still eyes, it wasn't like staring at death each day. There are no more mischievous waves churning, she smiles too much, and I want her to tell me a dirty joke just one more time like she used to and embarrass me. I want that feral thing back, for me and for her. She doesn't know, so I kiss her, and remind her, she's like that beautiful brave and bold rogue petunia swimming on her front porch towards light and the sun.

STEWART HAKOLA

Stones
for Steve

Since I changed my meds
my dreams are so vivid
waking up is hard to do, yet
Last night, you and Dad
were helping at my new house
20 miles north of Michigan Tech
where I just got a job as instructor
In this particular dream
My yard in this dream was a mess
(hey those might be flowers)
the neighborhood now impoverished
where agates in our pockets we were summer
You and Dad, you clear the shed as I run late
sweep it out, sweep the gravel off the sidewalk
pick the stones off the lawn, pile the best ones by
the porch to fill the cracks in the driveway the snow has left.

Where was Mom? And the Wives? (no Kids yet)
Did anyone at any time in this dream ever go inside?
(Yeah -- I did, I remember making beds for you and Dad
before we roll on, to the sandstone bars of Calumet)

Heroes of Socialist Labor

His right thumbnail was split in two
something about an ax on the farm or WWII
My high school history teacher was our neighbor
Father was at the Battle of the Bulge and more

I remember the shoebox in the basement, black and white
photos of the camps

She was first in her class at the Finn community college
served as secretary for the school's third president
After the war, the CFO of General Motors, then
the US Attorney. Mother taught me the bus downtown

I remember granite canyons, the US Courthouse, Hudson's
the row housed dominos of the poor (lock the car doors)

My hands are unscarred, I'm not blacklisted at the Soo Co-op
He finally did call her name, Maisie, at last
On my steering wheel, I see his hands
My sons, I take upon his lap

I remember crawling up on his Lazy Boy, forgetting
my friends were still there
When I was younger, a more dynamic attorney
I worked with GM's pro bono team
building cases for kids with disabilities
We saw some amazing things
(mom, I did an amazing thing)

I remember, after the hearing, the poor people
exiting tall buildings, driving to her house in the suburbs
my car windows all the way down

She had supper ready. Now she rests
The freeway shifts north
to the Finnish Center
and the cemetery, where
her urn stays
the pillow at his feet

Love's a quiet act
It rides the bus
It swings the ax

Deer Yards

They will walk in the deepening snow for many miles
passing through perfect conifer
to find their yard of cedar, of fifty years

We don't know why says the DNR
but there is one clue – you
would too

if you
were
safe
there
once
now again
fifty times in a row

that's several hundred human years

Pray

they are here for yours
to kill for generations

Finn Dog
for Alex

Finn in the woods
runs on ahead but
never leaves our sight
Finn in Harlow Lake
swims in a circle
for no reason
Finn rubs against me
I weep uncontrollably
(more than once)

Finn in Superior
drops stick one
under his chin
mouth free to
grab stick two
(a genius)

Finn noses my backpack
knows Ball is hidden
inside - good news
for the Finn dog

Finn in the sand
gyrating, allergic
Finn in the car, head
out the window
Two last trips with me
and the boys
To the beach – swim, please!
And then the vet's

Dear Finn bear
Buddy bear
Finnie
Finnie Barbarino
Sweetie
You can thank me later

The staff had lit candles – two
and Benny quoted Tolkien, I
said *woods* and *rivers*, over
and over while bright green
fields wait to receive you
The tech wraps your leg, she weeps
The leash snaps off – you're free!

Harlow Lake

“Nice pond,” he says

“I stopped at the DNR and said
'I am a water fowl hunter'”

“There’s a drop off,” I say

soon a 12-gauge wakes up Steve
dead geese bob out of reach
(glad Finn dog’s home at peace)

They’re gonna need a boat

He says “Nice talking to you”

“It was good to see you Stu”
My brothers break camp
two by two

After the water fowl
hunters came and went again
with their five geese
and their garish new
lime day-glo boat
from Walmart,
a “straight shot”
to suburban Chicago,
then I was really alone

ME KILPATRICK

Black Ashes with Prayer

I can't breathe –
Black ashes:
George Floyd's need,
the cross flashes.

I can't run from -
Black ashes:
Jesse Owens won,
hurdles and dashes.

I can't sing the blues –
Black ashes:
Holiday's "Strange Fruit" moves,
past white fascists.

I can't defeat-
Black ashes:
Rosa Park's seat,
as teeth gnashes.

I can't inspire –
Black ashes:
MLK took us higher,
Civil Rights passes.

I can't fight -
Black ashes:
Ali's human rights,
uppercut smashes.

I can't say it loud -
Black ashes:
"I'm Black And I'm Proud,"
the Godfather of Soul unlashes.

I can't grace -
Black ashes:
Arthur Ashe's place,
in tennis matches.

I can't dance and sing -
Black ashes:
Michael's "Billie Jean,"
the King of Pop snatches.

I can't jump -
Black ashes:
Air Jordan's dunks,
over racial clashes.

I can't talk -
Black ashes:
Oprah Winfrey knocks,
hearts open in masses.

I can't lead -
Black ashes:
Colin Kaepernick's knee,
where black lives flashes.

I can't erase -
Black ashes:
Bubba Wallace races,
past race flag hashes.

But I can retrace -
black ashes with prayer:
On one knee before race,
breathe peace into the air.

Marquette's Superior Voyage

I, Jacques Marquette, journeyed many waters,
following my French Jesuit superior's orders,
into dark and thick wooded forests,
in birch bark canoes that bore us.

I dreamt of the Indians of the Indies,
but it was the New France aborigines,
who took me on my superior voyage,
with canoe and cross in portage.

I learned their way of life,
and taught them Catholic rite,
and we communed in unity,
at each tribal community.

By canoe from Sault Ste. Marie,
they took me to the Mississippi,
with a French-Canadian explorer,
Christ-crossing New France's borders.

On the way back I got deadly sick,
in my dying hand my crucifix,
two years later they moved my bones,
and buried me in St Ignace by their homes.

Honoring my name after death,
Michigan's City of Marquette,
with statue giving Lake Superior shade,
at sunset for a superior voyage made.

The Mooching Moose

Looking out my cabin window,
Just outside a moose bent low,
chewing maple saplings by the row,
each munch he took so slow.

My breakfast guest looked up,
seeing me drinking from my coffee cup,
and realizing I did not interrupt,
he continued grazing in a grassy ruff.

He circled the family cabin staring in,
as if he wanted to make friends,
while also feasting maple leaves again,
my guest did not want his meal to end.

After a while when he got not a smile,
as he stood near the cabin wood pile,
cause the family dog barked wild,
the mooching moose vamoosed with style.

What is the Web We Have Spun?

The sinister spider's web is gone,
along with the victim won,
as the victor runs on,
my eyes spy spiders across the lawn.

Hanging webs spun on trees,
with struggling bugs begging pleas,
and upon this frightening frieze,
their executioners search and seize.

Do these lives matter at all?
They're just bugs with no justice call,
in a courtyard outside my barn stall,
I watch the scene depicting our fall.

What is the web we have spun -
the gory death from which we run,
where we make objects of everyone,
taking what we please when the pleas done?

The Web of Life

Pines, maples, and birch,
birthed by Mother Earth,
grow up from forest dirt,
as I do my Google search.

In this internet web of creation,
I find listings of information,
and see with fascination,
they miss their communication.

For words truly cannot describe,
the connection I feel inside,
when I look out the window besides,
with these trees where I reside.

For they offer me cool shade,
from the heat of the sun today,
even as I sit in a log cabin's glade,
built with family wood cut by blade.

Through the same window just outside,
another web displays a fight to survive,
a struggling creeper strung out to dry,
as a spider stings until the creeper dies.

I see the web of life before me,
with the will to last and be free,
as I grow up like these trees,
and not be trapped by enemies.

My UP Way of Life

Driving down the road in the UP,
all I see is road and trees,
a little breeze shakes the leaves,
as I leave worries behind me.

I love this country I live in,
as I drive around a bend,
Great Lake waves with ascend,
cause my head to spin.

I head down dirt roads by headlamp,
where in the wild woods I tramp,
park the truck and make camp,
and have dinner with Van Camp.

I get up with the campfire smoke,
and go skinny dip with friendly folk,
who offer me some of their toke,
but I'm already high from my UP soak.

I smell the flowers and the evergreen,
and watch the drama of an eagle scene,
as he swoops down to a fishing stream,
and snatches his trout catch clean.

I pack my backpack into the kayak,
with a tent and my food sack,
and with my paddle I leave no tracks,
as I wake the lake waters with a smack.

I look at the weather forecast,
after the lake woke up with wave blasts,
and see a crowd of clouds with windy gasps,
angry and upset I fear my kayak upcast.

The sky screams and the cloud cries,
but the downpour ends as I fight black flies,
but thank the UP gods for dragonflies,
as I recover with whelps on my thighs.

I continue my UP-life journey,
with no worry of a gurney,
for I'm in no hurry,
UP beauty shows me mercy.

I'm lucky if I see Northern Lights,
for they're heavenly sights,
but I'm lucky by all rights -
I breathe the UP day and night.

JESSE KOENIG

Silver Lining

Crossing the street.
One raindrop hit her forehead.
One big raindrop on an otherwise sunny day.

She stopped in her tracks.
She looked for birds.
Swabbed the substance off with her finger.
Sniffed it.
Stared at it.
Tested it for an explanation.

She smiled and looked up.
Searching for a rainbow.

In her peripheral,
a cloud formed.

And then it hit her.

Hit her like a bus.

Exactly like a bus.

Indeed, it was a bus.

And she lay in the road bleeding all over her favorite coat,
the one with the silver lining.

(A version of this first appeared in *Brief Perversions*, Burdock Press, 2015.)

The Dead Of Winter

The frozen ground was supposed to make it safe
To tell the stories
To speak the names

But the Dead of Winter
Have no flesh to freeze
No life to slow

In the thick, January, Upper Peninsula snow
The Dead of Winter sit in shadows
Look from picture window to picture window
Peering through open blinds, undrawn curtains
Glaring at the fireplaces and warm living rooms
Listening, planning

Between the first snowfall
And the first clap of thunder

The Dead of Winter
Possess snowmen
Flip off passing cars
Swat at birds that dare to land
Stab at pissing dogs with twig arms
Stare with glowing coal eyes

The Dead of Winter
Work secretly from under snow cover
Move below like burrowing animals
The surface rippling
Circling like sharks
Work the undercurrents
Guide sledfulls of children toward trees
Off cliffs
Trip toddlers
Pull them below

The Dead of Winter
Push down heavy on rafters
To hear them creak and strain
With the haunting
Drop icicles from roof edges
Stalactite daggers
Plunged through knit caps

…
In the back yard
The Dead of Winter
Throw snowballs from the forest edge
From just out of sight
Hidden at the edge of darkness
Beyond where the porch lights reach

Children look at each other for answers
They laugh nervously and call out the name of a neighbor kid
A prankster
A trickster
Knowing damn well Bobby or Jimmy could never throw like that
Throw that otherworldly far
And another snowball comes whirling out from the darkness

And another

And another

The Dead of Winter moan with the wind

I think I hear mother calling
It's time to go in

But one kid
A brave
Child
He squints to see through the falling flakes
Thinks he sees someone, something moving in and out
Forming and disappearing
Each time a gust kicks up snow in tiny tornados

His eyes go dark
And he begins a slow walk
Toward a rustle in the tree branches

His friends watch the shadows
Where his footprints end
Hesitantly call his name
What do you see?

And another snowball
A large one
Comes flying out from the dark woods

They follow it with wide eyes
As it rises
Arches high, disappears briefly
In the snowy night sky
Reappears on descent
For a second

Before falling at their feet

They look down, slack jawed
One lone boot
Settles before them
Wobbling
Like the awkward last turns of a spinning coin
And stops, laid out before them
Still warm
Melting snowflakes as they land

They stare and back away
Then run inside
Out of the Dead of Winter

Jonahs' Town

Smitty retired to the inside of a whale.

You may or may not remember the headline buried three pages into the daily news: "Two Dozen Whales Beached in Antarctica." You may have browsed right over the article, but Mr. Jonathon Rudipan McJarvis, entrepreneur extraordinaire—he did not. He had seen Best Marigold Hotel. He had an idea: cozy, all-inclusive, beach-front housing, for the rest of your life. And that's how he advertised it.

Now Mr. McJarvis, for all of his "great" ideas, was a penniless man. He showed up with little more than a knife and began construction. He began slowly, whittled with some hesitation, past failures fresh in his mind: mustache beads, wart puppets, three-way mirrors, medical slingshots,...

As the project proceeded, however, he forgot about all that was riding on it and returned to his true self—an artist. He gutted in a state of mania. He carved out decorative arches into the doorways. He used ice blocks to build elaborate foyers, no-season rooms. He shoveled winding pathways through snow sculptured yards, winding roads to nowhere with names like Wall Street, Campus Circle, Industrial Park Road, Cubical Way, Employment Dead End,...

Now Smitty, he and the other retirees dropped their suitcases in the snow where they stood and looked around them. Soon, they were huddled in a tight circle, talking amongst themselves. Although they had something much different in mind, they also had nothing to go back to. They were rejects from the world they had built, with their days in offices, factories, labs, ...

Jones spent 35 years teaching at a community college, scrimping by, living above his mother's garage, eating Ramen noodles, wiping his butt with junk mail. Disrespected by his students and the administration. But here, the others called him Professor. He liked it. They asked him what it feels like to freeze to death. He told them what he could remember from the Discovery Channel. They all nodded in agreement: There are worse ways to go.

So they settled in: Hung photos of dead family members from rib rafters. Arranged pillows and blankets out over tongue mattresses,...

The daily fires warmed up the insides of the whale, and they skimmed off their meals, down to the next frozen layer.

Two whales close together served as the commons area, where the ping-pong table, pool table, hot tub, bingo parlor... would never be.

There they gathered for community meetings, dealt with the needs of the village—gathering drift wood, extracting blubber for lanterns, scaring off scavenging birds,...

Davis worked security at a mall for a few years in her 30s. They never let her have a weapon, she was always chasing teenagers, and the local police constantly reminded her that she wasn't a real cop. Here, she was put in charge of the Neighborhood Watch: scheduling patrols, manning the lookout.

From the cliff, a village of two dozen whales. Frozen in mid flop. Nestled into the white, bleak landscape. Smoke coming out of blow holes. Lamplight escaping from small ice-windows jammed in here and there where eyes or blubber or genitalia used to be.

Home.

Around the perimeter, poles sticking out of the snow, remnants of the past skewered to each. A fence of impaled timecards, cell phones, car keys, watches, college degrees, membership cards, magazine subscriptions, credit cards, participation trophies, voter registration, leather wallets, Coach purses... Like decapitated heads on stakes.

A warning.

In the near distance, just over the rooftops, the frozen beach and open water.

They watched for cargo ships, research vessels, oil platforms, tankers, cruise ships,… invaders from another life.

The conch shell at the ready.

War paint applied.

They sharpened sticks and made their last stand.

Without Natural Affection

Anyone who does not provide for their relatives, and especially for their own household, has denied the faith and is worse than an unbeliever. (1 Timothy 5:8)

I hit the button and wait by the door. It's my turn, my shift. I check my reflection in the glass: It's all uniform and tattoos and muscles. I run a hand through my hair. The door unlocks with a clank, and I walk in.

It's not like in the movies: Some cool lookout tower, with us guards armed with rifles, searching the darkness with spotlights, past waves of barbed wire, looking for escapees. It's more like a doctor's office: Small. Sterile. It hums with florescent lighting. Grey concrete blocks in the walls. Light grey/dark grey squares alternate on the floor. This is where visitors wait, before we pass them through the metal detectorand, with a push of a button, they enter into the visiting area, to await their husband-, uncle-, cousin-, brother-gone-wrong, sporting the bright-orange jumpsuit of shame.

I walk up to the desk and drop my keys with a clatter. I take a quick look out the window into the waiting room. It's empty. I'm hanging my coat over the chair when I see Mario's got some documentary playing. It's the only screen not playing black and white security footage, so the color picture stands out; it catches my eye.

There's a Grizzly bear with her cubs meandering through the wilderness. It's a picturesque nature scene. And then—bam!—out of nowhere, some poor, unfortunate animal, maybe a woodchuck, not sure, pops out of its den and finds itself between the bear and her cubs, and suddenly it changes into a scene from a horror show: Blood and gore as mother bear goes apeshit on that thing, just tearing it apart.

I say, "Oh, damn!" out loud, to myself.

"Damn!": there's an echo behind me, where I hadn't noticed that Mario, packing up his belongings, sliding on his coat, had stopped to watch it too.

I look back at him.

"Oh, no. Oh, shit!" he continues, still looking at the carnage on the TV. Then he looks at me and shrugs. "Well, that's why you don't screw with a mother bear. She'll rip up anything she sees as a threat to her cubs. She'll put down her own life to protect them." He looks down briefly to zip up his coat. "She don't care. No fear. Just love. That's nature." He picks up his keys, slides them into his coat pocket, and he looks me right in the eyes. "Nothing more natural, more powerful than that love, that love of a mother."

I have to break his gaze, so I look back at the TV, where it's back to that pleasant nature scene: The happy family walking away. The cubs tumbling and wrestling, like nothing had happened, like Freddy Krueger hadn't just popped out of good old mom and murdered a random passerby.

As he passes behind me, Mario puts a hand on my shoulder. "I'll see you tomorrow."

Mario is nice, but I know he thinks I'm a weirdo. All these guys think I'm odd. I know it. I push the button and Mario slips out the door I had come in. It's not their fault. I never learned how to be normal. I turn the nob, and the TV goes off. I grab a magazine, but before I can settle into my chair, the outside door opens partially and a round face peeks though. "Good afternoon, Gordon. May I enter?"

"You know you can, Mrs. Everly."

As she shuffles through the door, she says, "Now, how many times have I told you, please, call me Edith."

The heavy door closes behind her with a loud click.

"I'm sorry. How are you today, Edith?"

"Oh, I am wonderful. Just wonderful. It's such a beautiful day. I thought I'd just stop by and surprise my sweet Martin. Is my boy available for visiting?"

It's unlikely to be a surprise, given that she's here pretty much every visitation day. I look at my list and see he hasn't lost his visitation privileges today. *Yet.*

I answer her: "Yes, Martin is available." I call it in.

Edith knows the protocol: Shoes off. Belt off. Hairpins out. Pockets emptied into the tray. Personal belongings into the locker.

"I sure hope they let my boy out in time for Thanksgiving. I'm making his favorite: Dark meat drumsticks slathered in gravy. Homemade cranberry sauce—not that stuff in a can, no, oh no. And pumpkin pie: A little warm still, with just a small dollop of whipped topping. Just like he likes it."

"Maybe, Edith." I say, "I hope so."

But I don't. I don't hope so. Her "sweet Martin" is a fucking psychopath. A real bad dude. Got a record a mile long. Mrs. Everly…Edith, I correct my thought, your boy has been bad, real bad. Just a matter of time before he gets transferred out of here and into max, where he belongs. I'm sorry, Edith, I think, but for the sake of all of society, it's best if your boy never sees another Thanksgiving in the outside world.

Edith walks through the metal detector and waits on the other side with her arms out. I hover a good foot and a half above her, and I have to bend down to run the wand around her.

"I sure do miss him" she says. She looks up from slipping her shoes back on and looks me in the eyes. "There's no love like the love of a mother for her child, Gordon, just nothing more true."

Seems like that's tonight's theme, I think, thinking back to the documentary and Mario earlier. I hand her her belt, and she takes it.

She asks, "Gordon, you gonna have a nice dinner with your momma?"

I stare for a while into those dark eyes, those caring orbs clouded with cataracts and unconditional love.

"Gordon?" she repeats.

"No," I clear my throat. "No, Edith… No… Just me."

Edith looks horrified. "Oh no, Gordon, how careless of me. Has she…Is she…Is your momma with Jesus?"

"No. She's not dead," I say. After a short pause, I surprise myself and add, "It's me. I'm dead."

Now, Edith, poor Edith looks very confused. I think she might be wondering if this is all a dream. Wondering if possibly she didn't get up from her bed this morning. That this isn't the passage to the visitation room, but instead the passage to the afterlife. She stares at me for an explanation.

"I'm dead. And she's with Jehovah."

Edith is more confused than ever.

"We don't talk. She won't talk to me. I'm not a Jehovah's Witness, so I'm dead to her."

She just stares some more. I'm getting uncomfortable.

"It's shunning. She won't talk to me anymore. Ever. Ever again. For the rest of my life."

She looks down to thread the belt through the belt loops in her pants. Shaking her head the entire time, saying, "Don't talk? Your Momma? Don't talk? Your Momma?" She finishes buckling her belt, and, with a concerned face, but a scolding finger waving up at me, she says, "Now, Gordon, whatever you did, you just call her up this very day and you tell her that you love her and that you miss her. She'll forgive you. And you'll be eating Turkey together like it ain't nothing. Like I said, there ain't nothing like a mother's love for her child. Ain't nothing."

I walk back to the desk and buzz the door to the visitation room. I'm not supposed to, but I walk back and hold the door for her.

"OK, Edith, I certainly will try." I say, just glad to be done with the conversation. "You have a great visit."

She gestures for me to come closer, like she has a secret to tell me. But when I bend in for a listen, she drops a kiss on my cheek.

I straighten up abruptly. She turns and walks away, into the visitation room. I guess I let go of the door because it shuts in my face and locks with a loud clank, and I just stare out the window into the visitation room.

I think: Did you know that Jeffrey Dahmer's dad visited him regularly in prison? His stepmom would fly out from California to visit him?

I don't know how long I'm standing there, but long enough for Martin to come into the visiting room. From the window, I watch Edith as she embraces her murderous madman with all her natural, unconditional, motherly love. It's a long embrace.

Eventually, I notice my own reflection in the glass. I turn away abruptly and quickly walk back to the desk, where I grab some tissues before anyone can see this grown-assed man, this prison guard crying 'cause he misses his mommy.

L. GAIL MAHAN

Medicine for the Soul

Remembered nights,
Whispers, sentiments

Childhood memories emerge

As musical notes drift
among figures transformed into spiritual beings –

a galaxy of souls

As drums beat, gyrating bodies move,
dancers spin and twirl, ingesting music's intoxicating fuel.

Figures drunk from an altar of notes
as they heal life's difficulties and hurts,
descending under a sea of soundwaves –

A medicine for the Soul.

Marilyn

A single bud blooming - becoming a bouquet of your mother's womb.
Plucked in your early years by a wonton soul.
Blood is drawn as a thorn pierces the skin.
Resilience persisted as petals spread their brilliance.

Your colorful beauty attracted onlookers.
Images held you captive as you sprouted into an eye pleasing bouquet.

Your spectral soul soared, bursting into stardom as your inner chamber yearned,
crying for spiritual honey.

Petals dropped as depression imprisoned your soul,
falling into sleepless nights and endless days.
Tossed by the winds of time, crushing and mangling delicate petals of soul.
Seeking solace, addiction became your living water,
created to free you from self-imposed demons, wilting your stem of perseverance.

You became a victim, craving nectar of euphoria.

Sleep drooped your head wilting your leaves of strength as petals of willpower
dropped, summoning the "Angel of Death".

We The People

We the People gathered herbs and berries.
We planted corn and squash.
We grind our corn and gather honey for the kneel down bread.

We the People pray and give offerings to our Creator.
Our homes are round like Mother Earth.
Our Creator blesses us with all our needs as we live in harmony
with Mother Nature.

We the People hunt wild game and thank them and our Creator
for their gift to us.

We the People became a nation of government dependence
when our land was taken, no longer allowed to hunt,
fish freely or gather for our needs.

We the People weep for our young.
Our Elders pray for our indigenous nations.

We the People – through tears watched our young take because
We did not understand your God.

We the People have abandoned our way of life
to become a people of your way of life.

MATT MAKI

Not Beautiful

Ukraine, 24 February 2022, 8th year & 1st day of war

I'm sorry this isn't a beautiful poem,
but what have you done to deserve something beautiful?
I had sat down to write about a perfect cup of coffee
and what I see in its cream and froth,
but the air raid sirens are distracting.
Eight years of this and getting worse,
but you only now care about it.
In that time, what have you done to try to stop it?
Let's excuse the previous ten years of warnings
because news is confusing, and there is a lot of it,
and it isn't clear what will mean what.
But this war started eight years ago,
and all of these things: invasion, tanks,
rape, looting, deportations and vanishings,
propaganda, international election meddling,
missiles, evening news announcements
of threats to use nuclear and chemical weapons.
A slow local news day is the only reason
you're paying attention now; it's either this
or a new Supreme Court judge.
So no, you haven't earned something beautiful.
You barely even deserve the truth,
but that's what I'll give you here nevertheless.

I'm Sorry

Ukraine, 5 March 2022, 8th year & 10th day of war

I'm sorry for jogging one sunny morning.
I'm sorry I'm still working when you have lost your job.
I'm sorry you need to show me how to ribbon old clothes and weave them into camo nets,
and sorry I wasn't here sooner.
I'm sorry I'm worried about the money I'm losing in the plunging exchange rate instead of buying medicine and body armor for you.
I'm sorry for panicking in the empty supermarket when you are waiting in line for a bag of donated cooking oil and pasta.
I'm sorry I never renewed my driver's license and can't drive you out of here.
I'm sorry for worrying about the emotional well-being of my teammates two to ten countries away in their refugee hotels.
I'm sorry for choosing to stay when you would choose to leave.
I'm sorry for feeling good about my choices.
I'm sorry for my poor sleep in an apartment of snoring evacuees when you are sleeping in a bomb shelter with a thousand strangers.

I'm sorry for not wearing my mask, thinking it no longer matters.
I'm sorry for judging whether things matter.
I'm sorry for buying razors, a bath mat, cookies, a t-shirt, and finally Q-tips with sturdy cardboard stems and not flimsy plastic.
I'm sorry for caring about petty conflicts at work.
I'm sorry for using internet when you are cut off in your bunker.
I'm sorry.
I'm sorry for eating in restaurants and feeling good about my generous tips.
I'm sorry for feeling my feelings.
I'm sorry for caring about how the news is being reported almost as much as what is being reported.
I'm sorry for sharing with my international friends which sanctioned companies they should boycott instead of more photos of murdered babies.
I'm sorry for charging my devices.
I'm sorry for doing laundry.
I'm sorry I didn't speak more with those colleagues and acquaintances who've been murdered and sorry for wishing I could claim their loss as my own.
I'm sorry for going to the mall.
I'm sorry for enjoying today's weather.
I'm sorry I hadn't written anything to inspire Putin's assassination or at least dissuade russians' blind worship of him.
I'm sorry I bought a Lion bar. I realized too late that it is by Nestlé. I'm sorry for thinking that throwing it in the trash would help.
I'm sorry for doomscrolling instead of getting out there and actually doing something.
I'm sorry I still haven't learned the language well enough to be an asset rather than a potential liability in a crisis.
I'm sorry for being distracted and not taking advantage of this inspiring moment to write, and sorry to take advantage of this situation to write.
I'm sorry for drinking a Coke without knowing it was on the boycott list.
I'm sorry for recommending friends donate to the Red Cross and thereby enabling the forced abduction of 18,000 Ukrainians to russia.
I'm sorry for sleeping in during my days off.
I'm sorry for drinking the Mountain Dew my friend Tanya brought me back from her U.S. trip.
I'm sorry for inviting my Kyiv friends to come out of their shelters to hang out with me because I missed them.
I'm sorry for convincing my personal trainer to resume our street workouts every other day on his breaks from guarding the blockade in the Territorial Defense.
I'm sorry for celebrating my birthday.
I'm sorry.

The Selfishness of War

Ukraine, 20 March 2022, 8th year & 25th day of war

The worst part of war
is not being able to complain.
If the missile strikes terrify the kids
and make your weeks sleepless,
someone else has been hit by
that missile, so you have the best of it.
If your windows splinter throughout your home
and across your skin and eyes,
someone else had their home pulverized.
If the cold granite floor of the bomb shelter
is impossible to sleep on,
someone else is lying on the curb with a
bullet to the back of their head
as they were running to reach that shelter.
If your children are struggling to eat
gummy pasta simply soaked in cold water,
another parent watches her children waste away
and die after a week of no food.
If it looks like a monster has taken a bit
out of each building in your neighborhood,
someone else's city is flattened rubble.
If you haven't been able to reach your parents
for three weeks since the phone grid went down,
someone else found their parents' bodies.
If you've caught Covid in the bomb shelter
and have no possibility for medicine,
someone else caught it too but needs a ventilator.
If your work is disrupted by no wifi each time
every day you need to go to the bomb shelter,
someone else lost their job and income,
and someone else had their store obliterated.
If you stink from an unshowered week
and you have no toothbrush,
someone else has already been so for a month
but doesn't notice among the stench of
the nearby dead.
If you were abducted and beaten,
someone else was too and also raped.
If you were raped,
someone else is still being raped.
If you are still being raped,
someone else is too but in front of their child.

To Cope

Ukraine, 5 April 2022, 8th year & 41st day of war

To cope, I imagine I am a pet
left behind, lying in front
of what was once our building
waiting for it to be home again,
or picking among the rubble
to find where there was some kitchen,
because that's about all
I can handle now, the raw
fear and confusion and loneliness.
Please don't ask me
to solve all this somehow.
I won't inventory my complaints here
since they can't compare
to the horrors of even my neighbors.
I try to help how I can
but I can barely even help myself.
About all the energy I have
is enough to emit a pitiable sound,
turn around three times,
lie down here,
and wait.

Compromising Heaven

Ukraine, 3 June 2022, 8th year & 100th day of war

I hope that Heaven
isn't an endless snowy field
where we, bundled in animal
souls against the wind,
trudge silently through
muffled snowdrifts.
Maybe it will be.
Not everyone agrees
what comprises paradise,
so probably the majority
will have to be disappointed.

GALA MALHERBE

Trapper's Lake

Let me stand beside you, friend,
as silent and still as cedar on this wild shore,
as if to call the kingfisher in at the end of the day.
Let me stand beside you, friend, as we wait
for the hollow song of the hermit thrush
to land in our chests just after the sun dips
behind hemlock, a breath beyond the final glow,
as the flame of the eastern shore flickers,
leaves calm water to whirly bug and merganser.
Let us stand together, feel the pause between stanzas,
that sacred space large enough for hope, for faith.
At last, let us understand grace.

L'espérance

(French for *hope.*)

Mirabel moon rises over stucco and shutter, over
rouge float of geranium, over violet trumpets of hibiscus,
over bees asleep in stump and wall, pale pollen
still coating their soft sweater vests. Swallows dive and dart,
invisible, follow the mayflies, their one-day lives,
give meaning to death, save them from feather graves
in morning crevices of bridge and bench.
Music fills this park, reaches chestnut and basswood, unites
young and old as locals watch from tables and chairs.
The drummer keeps the beat. The guitarists face one another
and jam. The singer grasps her mic, inhales hardship…
exhales celebration and joy- Elvis, Bon Jovi, Midnight Oil,
sings in English, her accent unmasked. A community claps and sways.
A woman raises her arms. Suddenly I feel it—hope, l'espérance
right here in this village in Les Ardennes, more than a year later.

Family Reunion with Aunt Pauline

We gather, each August, in the pines,
under the pavilion, near the horseshoe pits.
In the field, someone has placed picnic tables,
end to end, 12 tables, maybe more,
spread the family tree from one to the next,
a continuous document of lineage,
of marriages and deaths, of births and family units.
Standing on its end it would be as tall as these white pines
that surround us as we bend over names and dates and history.

I strum my guitar beside my dad and my uncle,
beside relatives I do not know. I watch fingers
for chord changes. I look over at Aunt Pauline.
She sings along to *Five Foot Two* beneath her flowered hat
from her lawn chair. A paper plate rests on her lap,
a half-eaten piece of birthday cake. She is 104 this year.

After the singing, I follow her to the outhouse.
She pushes her walker over grass and roots.
I become a vigilant guardian behind her.
My arms hover close, out-stretched and ready.
She pauses, looks up at the pines, tells me,
"I remember when these were just this high."
She gestures shoulder height with her hand.

I wonder if this could be true, then I think of that family tree
rolled out like a red carpet in the field. So often,
we are poor believers in size, in age, in the power of time.

For this afternoon, I am content to walk my great-aunt
back from the outhouse among white pines
just a few years her elder. I imagine us both
in our flowered hats, sauntering down the red carpet
of our shared family tree.

Instead

I sit on this metal swing on a late June morning
beneath mock orange, bent full with sweet citrus,
porcelain white, a few petals already tinged
with the rust of farewell. Beside me, lavender sprigs,
pruned last evening splay crisscrossed, like pick-up sticks,
smell like summer, remind me of Provence, of hillside fields,
lavender billows, warm wind, painted light, waves of violet-blue,
of olive trees and spice merchants, of French Provincial cloths
hung 'round a street vendor, stucco walls, the color of salmon,
the Mediterranean churned turquoise against a chiseled shore,
bougainvillea, thick as magenta moss stretched to rooftops as if
to seek entry through shuttered windows, not unlike
my own emotions, lined up at the doorway of my locked heart,
pacing the cobbled street of my despair, hollow cups held skyward
to catch my tears, wanting only a turn to be felt. But instead,
I sit quietly in the garden, rehearse my tasks: stake the sunflower,
train the beans, free the butterfly weed from the bergamot,
this silent community of growth far easier to manage
than the unsolved riddles of my soul... all these puzzles in my heart.

Transformation

A lake halted, mid-breath,
nothing smoother, more solid,
more secure than that glossed surface
that held us like miracles, like prophets,
as we balanced on silver blades,
etched spirals, loops, sine waves
into a sunset sky, into the mirror
of those moments, our bodies freed
to dance like spilled mercury,
our pink cheeks full with living,
as we circled again and again
around a frozen sun,
as if we had wings.

Today

In this pure lavender dawn, a full moon
sets over The Smokies. Ridges draw shapes
on the horizon. I argue with my friend
over to be or not to be... a Buddhist...
of all things, because attachment
or optimism, whatever we choose,
does our eight-fold path or our baptism
really matter at all if we are awake enough
to see wren and song sparrow,
arbutus and anemone,
far off tulip poplars and sweet gum
as they sprout like soft fur on the neck
of an uneasy dog, who deep down
really only wants to run free
through forest or field, nuzzle
through dry leaves for scat or death,
does not want to be bothered
by challenge or threat, especially
on a day when mist hangs like mystery
and grass grows as green as Ireland.
Not today, says the dog, who only wants
to feel contentment in his bones, become
as simple and sweet as moss as it billows
in sycamore and trillium groves in March.

BEVERLY MATHERNE

Fusion

for Roger Magnuson

Famine kiss, serpentine embrace,
The joy of it all. How did two specks
In the universe collide, hold so fast?

(Previously published in *Verbal Art: A Global Journal Devoted to Poets and Poetry* (2020) Vol. 4, Issue 2.)

The Gift

for Roger Magnuson

That morning, you awoke thirsty. I couldn't give
You enough water. You tried to stand
At your bedside but collapsed. Prostrate, you stared
At the ceiling, your eyes glassing over.
The EMTs carried you out the front door,
Down ice-glazed steps, one stone unstable,
Throwing them off balance. Truck doors swallowed
Your body. I didn't know whether I'd see you again.

I hold you in a meadow of trillium, in Munising,
Marsh Marigolds ablaze along the narrow country road,
Kiss you in the tenderest way I know.

(Previously published in *Verbal Art: A Global Journal Devoted to Poets and Poetry* (2021) Vol. 5, Issue 1.)

Dear Greta Thunberg,

When you address complacent elders, some of whom don't even accept global warming, when you hurl, "Don't you dare leave me with a broken planet," I ride your tsunami, shiver before your power to change the world.

I wonder, too, Greta, whether you might have a russet puppy at home, or a bunny, all white, except for black paws. Might you call him Toby, roll onto your back on the floor, knees bent, hold him high in the air, bring him down fast, up in the air and down, up and down, the way a doting mother does her toddler, the little one squealing, you crying: "I love you, Toby! I love you, Toby!"

Sincerely,
Beverly Matherne

Dear Karen,

When you were little, before you walked, I fed you soft-boiled eggs for breakfast, placed the spoon in my own mouth, sculpting its contents to slide onto your tongue. As a little girl, you ran to me whenever you hurt yourself or someone hurt you. I would hold you until you calmed. When you turned 16, I introduced you to Holden Caufield. You fell in love the way I had.

All-around smartie, beautiful writer, you taught gifted and talented students, watched them become teachers, engineers, business executives. Sometimes, your charges turned to drugs, and you told me about the one who overdosed. You grieved for him, his grandmother, all those who lost their way. "So much talent, so much talent," you always said.

When you turned 18, you called me from your dorm room to say you were getting married. All semester, for $2.00 an hour, I worked in the Registrar's Office at Saint Louis University, where I was a student, to earn my airfare. When Anjeanette, your first-born, came into the world, you named me Godmother. When your husband Cheeky got cancer, I went back home, to hold you, reminisce with him, how, when I had finished my Ph.D., the two of you had come with that little U-Haul trailer to fetch my books and me.

We saw a Victorian melodrama on a riverboat, got dizzy atop the Gateway to the West. On campus, we made rounds through Romanesque Cupples House, purple sandstone, mythical beasts at rainspouts, copper towers. Inside, Celtic carvings, Tiffany windows, 42 rooms in all. Before heading home, Mass at St. Francis Xavier College Church, where we marveled at fanned vaults, Gothic arches. Like stained-glass windows at Chartres in France, ocean blue bathed pink granite columns, the Altar, and us, taste of celestial.

Today, retired from teaching, we cherish visits year after year. Share losses, too, our brothers June, Albert, Johnny, Dennis; our sister, Emily; Daddy, Mama. My last birthday, my 75th, you thanked me for making you my pet cat as we grew up, and, through it all, you've loved me back. Old Faithfuls, Old Faithfuls, that's what we are.

Your loving sister,
Beverly

Were-Coon
Inspired by "Were-Coon," a painting by Simon Alleman

My name is Clovis Coon, but it should be Perfect Omnivorous Eating Machine because my greatest obsession is food, food, food, all year round, food.

Here, in the swamp, I get tired of bullfrogs, crawfish, worms, so in early spring, I head to town. There's nothing like road kill, like lapping up the splat of a dead rat or doe.

As weather gets warmer and skies bluer, I raid backyard gardens, small fields, before everything gets canned for winter, or picked over for the French Market.

In March, my middle name is Ravenous. I devour all the young asparagus shoots, all the cauliflower I want. By April, I'm foraging beets and cabbage. By May, I'm laying waste blueberry bushes, carrying off eggplants, cucs. You'll see me plundering the blackberry patch in June, paws and mug stained purple.

I'm gathering figs by August, some sour and rotting. Umm. I'm looting the grapevines, give me the rancid grapes. Give me the over-ripe watermelon, covered with mold. I'm razing the corn patch, give me kernels, fat and crunchy. In September, October, I'm demolishing collard greens, digging for yams. I'm pillaging persimmons in November; in December, parsnips, clementines.

And give me nuts, nuts, nuts, my favorite. They fatten me best for winter. I get all the acorns I want in the swamp, but here, in town, I'm ransacking cupboards and pantries for pecans, filberts. I'm raiding groves, once aphids set in, caterpillars and larva set in, boring holes in shells.

Now, it's February and my cousin, Alphonse Coon, invites me to a king cake party in New Orleans. Well, I already got a natural mask. Who's going to know whether I'm a raccoon or a petit Frenchman in disguise? I get there, and all along the back wall of the dance hall are king cakes. "Don't give me a little bitty piece," I say to myself, and run away with a whole cake, the one containing the Baby Jesus, it so happens. I devour it, its oodles of frosting, purple, green, and gold, under the full moon, my favorite prowling time.

The moon strokes my fur, settles like doubloons in my black eyes. I bury my nose in its beams, gulp them like thick honey, until I feel the white breath of Midas on my body.

Next thing I know, I'm morphing into something I'm not. I'm growing taller. Something's happening to my ears, they're relocating, to the sides of my head, like a human's. My teeth are getting bigger and sharper, my nails, normally petit and pointy, are getting longer and more hooked, like Madame Grands-Doigts' claws. I see witches flying about, bats darting, wolves howling. I'm chasing after Cajun boys and girls, the ones who tell lies, steal toys, stay out too late at night.

Then I see the fiddler heading home after the dance. I'm right on his heels, biting his butt. Blood, blood, give me blood. I'm piercing his neck with my big canines, sucking more blood, suck, suck, all I can get.

I let him go, collapse, conk out a bit. When I wake, it's morning, and I'm so tired I can hardly walk home, but I do. I stumble up the road, into the swamp, craving moss and sleep. Bullfrogs drill my ears. I sniff the muddy air and vaguely remember something about sweet cake, frosting, and a tiny baby, its moon face smiling down on me from the stars.

ROSLYN ELENA McGRATH

How to Find a Poet

Follow the trail of stardust
peeking from edges of pebbles
and pockets and peanut butter,
keeping a sharp eye out
for bits of fishing line.

Listen for high-pitched cries
for help punctuated
by peals of laughter, simmering
alliteration, the hush
between thoughts.

Toss out handfuls of shimmering
confetti, eerie
reflections, and whimsical
lullabies as bait.

Putter.

Play music.

Play with babies.

Sing.

Nap.

Have a good time.

Complain vociferously.

Forget about finding a poet,
or a petunia, or a pot to piss in.

A poet and poetry will join
you when ready.

Constellation

Caught like a grain of sand in the endless
ocean of sky skewered
by traces of a fine, far-off net
of flickering ancient light,
I lie slack-jawed in its inseparable grasp.

For Hans Hoffmann

With each layer of paint that grew
worlds of form and color beyond
gravity's pull, a dolphin
spun on its axis, somersaulted
through blue skies, dove
beneath deeper blue
with a flip and a whip and a whoosh
of back-bending delight.

You would respond with even more saturated
hues, your brush echoing the slap
of dolphin tail on water as it gorged
the eight-foot canvas with more wet paint.

I could lie down on the smooth
tiled floor or sun-warmed sand, breathe
your effervescence forever.

Honey

Honey, your golden glow clings
to whatever you touch, bringing sweetness
distilled from the center of sun
and soil's love child with fuzzy yellow pellets
flown on armadas of buzzing
feet to serve the queen,
perpetuate a species, a climate, a land,
fanned into viscous treasure to pour
onto bread and into batter,
a gold mine of sustenance.

Blessing

Bless the light that silvers
the sliver of moon, dapples
through woods, breaks
waves into diamonds.

Bless the waters
that move the shine
in this light, go deeper
than darkness, flow
through earth, tree, armpits, urine,
are exhaled up
to cloud swirls, rain down
on thirsty lands, cold concrete,
withered souls, hungry hands.

Bless the wind that moves
the waters, hustles bright
leaves to far corners, carries
cold, warm, and wet to new
territory, reminds us to change.

Bless the soil that shines with loam,
minerals, ant hill, deer pee, worm glow,
breathes its treasures into veins
of briar root, bird's tree, squirrel's home.

Bless the fire that boils
deep within the earth, creates
magma, blow holes, burns
in our hearts, blazes
through hearths, homes, and pits.

Bless the sounds that wake
us from slumber, clap
us to attention, breathe song
through lips, hands, ear drums.

Bless the musicians who corral sound
into poetry, poetry into visions,
visions into movement,
movement into silence that slips
through souls.

Bless all.

CAROLYN McMANIS

Field of Flowers

I am lying in a field of flowers
    Soft petals caress my skin
    All will be alright

I am bleeding in a field of flowers
    Thorns prick my heart and veins
    Blood pools around my brain

I am suffocating in a field of flowers
    Cloying pollen steals my breath
    I gasp for air

I am drowning in a field of flowers
    Sweet nectar fills my lungs
    All is still

I am decaying in a field of flowers
    Roots absorb my ashes
    I am one with the earth

I am soaring above a field of flowers
    Bright colors tether my soul
    I must fly free

White Privilege

I've never had to teach my son to fear
The men in blue upholding rule of law
Our nation's laws protect those I hold dear
It's in their practice that we find the flaw

I've never had to lie awake at night
And wonder if my son will be shot dead
Because his skin is black or brown, not white,
And guilt's assumed, force used to snip life's thread

Yet mothers 'cross this nation know the score:
Our children are not equal in this land,
A truth which rocks our country to the core
And forces us to take a moral stand

I ask myself: when will our country change
And justice be for all, not just in name?

In a Box

I put my anger in a box

> The loss of social interactions
> A dysfunctional government
> Unsupportive co-workers
> A world wracked by disease

Eventually it escapes
Blowing off the top, bursting through the walls
Until only splinters remain

I put my grief in a box

> The loss of my father
> The dysfunction of my mother
> A job I no longer recognize
> My vision of the world shattered

Eventually it escapes
Tears flowing over the edges, through the seams
Until only a puddle remains

I put myself in a box

The New Normal

There is nothing normal about "the new normal"

Face masks
Stay at home orders
Work from home
Shops closed
Social distancing

We do not live in "unprecedented times"

Bubonic Plague
Cholera
Influenza
HIV/AIDS
Corona virus

We are not "all in this together"

Economic disparity
Lack of health care
Pre-existing conditions
Homelessness
Racism

There is nothing normal about "the new normal"

COVID-19 Blues

Woke up this morning, sun high in the sky
Thought about getting up, but then I wondered why
I got the blues
The no reason to get up COVID-19 blues
If I sleep until noon, it'll still be too soon, wake me next June
COVID-19 blues

Grabbed me some coffee, walked around in a daze
Is it May? Is it June? Is it Monday? My mind is in a haze
I got the blues
The foggy, confused COVID-19 blues
The weeks are a blur, I have to endure, oh please find a cure
COVID-19 blues

Did some stress baking, a loaf of French bread
Changed my mind about cooking, gobbled two Poptarts instead
I got the blues
The what should I do COVID-19 blues
No yeast to be found, junk food abounds, put on a few pounds
COVID-19 blues

Took a walk along Third Street, it's like a ghost town
The shops are all closed with no one else around
I got the blues
The nowhere to go COVID-19 blues
I feel so alone as I aimlessly roam, I should just go home
COVID-19 blues

Went to a meeting, of course, it's on Zoom
Forgot to hit mute as I curse this unnatural room
I got the blues
The virtual meeting COVID-19 blues
Froze once, pooped out twice, confounded device, frustration's the price
COVID-19 blues

The virus continues, is there no end in sight?
Back at work now, I just hope it will be alright
I got the blues
The country opening COVID-19 blues
Stay six feet away, we might be okay, oh please go away
COVID-19 blues

ELLA MIDDLETON

The Beach Stretches Down

I was watchin' you one day.

Your white shape workin' down the beach. Bendin' and movin' with the waves. Pickin' up rocks and puttin' em' back down.

The way your hands were,
The way your hands were looked like they might drop something silver into my hand, like they might bring something up from the waves for me.

But each rock found your pocket, and your jacket grew heavy.
So I said thank you, Turnin' on my heel.

And found my path in the other direction.

The Woods Today

The flitting shadows trace daylight on my fingertips,
Prancing shadows on the cat's paw. Stiller still. On dusty winds, the leaves are carried.
Indulgent hues, these fleeting summer flecks, are passing time on worm-ridden logs.

The Cold Months

We attempt to start over, in winter.
Our weary feet dragging, yearning to be set down.
We are ready to sleep. To come into contact with our humanity,
the cold makes sure of that.
The world digs deep into the earth, to rest, to gather strength, to take time.
The frozen ponds, dry reeds, frogs, and fish, all gone to sleep.
But us humans are awake, to greet the frosted sunsets, the meet the waning light
yet we hibernate too, by our fires, under our blankets,
waiting for spring.

SUSAN A. MORGAN

Burying a Finn

for Evert Hakola, 1914 -1988

On that day you sat bone stiff like Rudyard limestone, south of Sault –
back stacked rock on rock, your mouth the thin curved line of ore
humped black for winding miles. Staring straight
blue as Pastor's words dropped down, bounced up
like rain on fields once robbed of stone.

That shiny suit. Those stiff black shoes. You leaned hard,
left a space between us because – I thought – I cried.
I still think so. I had not learned the language of this place.

Later, in a drunken outburst,
your mother's tongue split open: "A good man. He was a good man!" Her words
were sharp, they rattled loose somehow,
rushing out away from her the way this lake will quest
and spin until it finds a level. They startled me.

As if someone had argued.

Drought: 22nd July 1987

Our garden is dry. I coddle hollyhocks and tomatoes, sprinkle them early before
the sun can rob the earth.

Big-bellied women carry water, hanging before them like gourds
My womb gushed forth one day when it could hold no more.

It may rain soon, they say, Saturday, perhaps. Here,
The sky is so thin the blue bleeds
to eggshell, the membrane of nest robbed by crows.

Noah, his father named him. After the flood
when they placed him in my lap, it was sore – his skin
frayed tender – worn away like toes too long in a tub.

We are duped by the speech of the weathermen who spin a conundrum of hope –
"partly cloudy" promises more sun than shade.

His limp, starved limbs, his hands, his dimpled knee. Eyes sealed shut in mute grace.
How could such a perfect mouth refuse to take up milk?

The peas are falling. The pods are stopped half-full and rattle hollow music.

The nurse asked me "have you had enough time?"

On our lawn, I call to the neighbor boys as they chase one another with squirt guns dripping
– the impossible curve of their ribs – I beg them to drown me where I stand.

We can never have enough love.
I carry buckets one by one to the garden gate.

Deeryards

I

Somewhere west of Custer
I-90 spills onto open prairie.
Tourists huddle on cedar planks
designed for viewing.

A buffalo! my mother cries.

We cup our hands to shield our eyes…
remorseless glare of sun on grass, teacup
sky bleeds blue to eggshell, pale at the margins.
Leached of mercy.

You can see forever! my father exclaims.

Tell me, would you know
The hour of your ending?

II

At Harlow Lake fog drifts
in and between matchstick stands
of spruce and hemlock, pools and drapes us
in heavy damask.
We wait a thin dawn.

Watch, my husband whispers.

If you would see,
conform sight to expectation:
curved bow of spine and muscled neck,
knees lifting over snow in supple grace.
Spiked lash and sooted lips.

The tail a blaze of white, sharp
crack of shot.

Leaving Forest

When we were children, my mother,
my father, my sisters, and me,
in the middle –
faced forward, faced back,
rattling like vagabonds,
on the long, loose seats of our '63 Ford

We headed west, away
from cool waters and
Michigan forests. The trees
smudged a spruce-dark horizon.

On Dakota plains

the nodding sweep of wheat-spread arms stretched wide from day
toward night, a sky so broad it cracked, crazed leather.

I leaned across my sister's legs and watched for hours, the way a hawk will dip and wheel
and stitch desire to pulse and blood – lull
the ground and ride the sweep of fierce
air to earth.

I imagined him there with talons curved and gripped into the matted forbs
and grasses, the weave so dense
it gave its bones up to the air
and watched them scatter to bleach on
pioneer soil.

A remnant, the ranger told us,
brave in the face of fire and resurrection.

He told us, then, of the Pishko bird,
Who flies and flies and dips and glides
Over hills and plains and on to Orion,
searching for a lost and empty nest.

And I thought how we,
accustomed to the sanctuary of trees
and easy cover, might learn to live
as prairie.

Might shift a wing to echo
the blue-bowl arc of sky,
swell to fit its generous curves,
our skin so smooth
that bones would lose their limits

JANE PIIRTO

Social Distance

Every person buried or burned,
murdered or diseased, returns
by process, to soil.
In these days of tantrums
by presidents, accusations
by races, conflict
by nations asserting rights, pleas
by the starving, the laid off,
the ill, the bereft, unfairly chosen
by circumstance and bad luck,
I choose to remember the ball of tinfoil,
of string, holes in darned socks
the folded piles of last year's wrapping paper,
bacon fat in a tin can, bread heels in warm milk,
the simple thrift of a housewife and worker,
with ambitions for their children
to graduate from college and do well.

Once on Christmas Eve
in the early 1950s
after sauna and *lipia kala* at Grandma's,
my uncles and aunts gathered
in our kitchen, drinking,
singing, laughing, talking loud,
while we cousins were sent to sleep upstairs.

The glow of their camaraderie
seems overwhelmingly nostalgic
in a wildfire world
where solitude prevents,
masks muffle our lucid, gesturing eyes,
mutes the dampened amplification
of seasonal memory.

I live alone now,
struggle to feel joy
while the body count climbs,
beyond the precarious barrier
of my front door.

God Checks Email

What? 2 billion since last night before I went to sleep?
          Oh. I never sleep. Just kidding.

They click in and in and in constantly.
I must change my sounds and haptics.
Vibrate Only is jiggling my belly.

Yes. There is a Santa Claus. Virginia, listen to me.
You thought that God and Santa Claus are different?
All is One.

Even I have to unsubscribe from political parties' fund-raising asks.
Even I am in those begging loops from candidates.
Even I don't know if they are worthy. "Chip in," they say.
I don't have a credit card or a bank account and I don't play favorites, you know?

What? India's farmers are emailing me again?
I thought I told Shiva to not .cc me.
The Rohynga are being killed and enslaved in western China?
First they exile my friend the Dalai Lama from Tibet; now this.
Myanmar? Aung Song Suu Kyi? Didn't they give her a Nobel Peace Prize?

Tell Buddha.
Jesus wept.

I'm busy enough with that Texas border situation and those lost kids.
And now it's fire season and heat waves and another drought out west.
There will be more long rifle massacres, even some in my name. Watch this space.

And the Middle East.
Women can't drive cars in Saudi Arabia. It's true. It kills me.
Palestinian hide tunnels. Rockets and bombs burst in air
again and again and again.
Yes, it is all about me. It is. Call me Allah. Or Jehovah. Gaia will do.

Since people stopped kneeling and thinking thoughts to bend to me,
now they're beginning to text, as well. More to check.
It's hard to intuit their voices when they text.

What? 1.5 billion new texts and emails in the last 15 minutes?
I'm an omniscient omnipresent God, but how can even I cope?
Priorities, people. Don't ask me to help you win your basketball game.

White Birds On A Sand Bar

Longing for the eternal
in Yeats' "white birds" poem.
The motif of birds a constant
burning ache for communion.
The arc that leads to wisdom.

The third world of the poem
brings the deep psychology
of subtle underchoices.
A spirit of discernment,
flame of the ages' sages—

In 2019 people swam in Marquette
at the mouth of Le Riviere du Mort,
near the industrial sculptured
pocket ore dock that loomed
as if the water were deep.
It wasn't.

The sand bar now there was as hidden
as forgotten yearning.
The Riviere du Mort has revealed a new mouth.
Now the herring gulls preen,
saunter with buoyancy,
mate, bicker, parent, pick,
Where the water used to be too deep.

We took off our masks
as if 2 years of roils,
almost a million deaths,
the lurking invisible virus,
the heavy toll of storm-wrought
erosion hadn't occurred.

Going maskless to gatherings,
we almost forgot the fear
before the jabs, as if we denied
the inevitability of transformation.
If you can dream you can write poems.
What is under eventually realizes in each of us.

Did you know that New York's
Hudson Bay's Oyster Island
surfaced in May 2021's full moon
for two hours at a rare very low tide
long enough for a picnic
and scientists' rapid exploration;
then it sank beneath again?

Submerged islands full of white birds reappear
when moon, storm, tide, and currents merge,
forced by the windborne fickleness of sand,
the sober frolics of white birds,
and a studied decision about
science's prophetic insight.

The Lilacs Of Ishpeming

Every year the second week of June
welcomes an explosion of lavenders,
a riotous splendor of survival.
Coexistent with forget-me-nots and apple blossoms,
old lilacs open in old yards near rundown houses
Cleveland, New York Locations, mines now closed;
in unkempt yards near derelict houses.

Syringa vulgaris, sturdy and stubborn,
staying alive rendering beauty.
Banks. Clouds. Mounds. Masses.
Bundles. Hills. Dunes, clumps, of lilacs.
The dapple of blooms overruns
dilapidated shacks, leans over aged fences.
Amethyst cones. Plum shafts.

Drive into the abandoned neighborhoods
of Negaunee on Merry Street
where sinking ground
made the homeowners flee.
Steps with no porches
lead to thickets of bushes grown to trees.
Yellow swallowtail butterflies dart.

Walk the path along Lake Superior.
Tiers and verges. Borders shore the shore.
Appropriately, French lilacs thrive
in the rocky Father Marquette Park.
And the air! Sniff the essence,
distill summer's advent.
Put it to your nose. Remember.

Girls used to plan their weddings
for this week. They filled the altars with
these blooming canes and branches
their heart-shaped leaves green as ivy,
a verdant quintessence,
blessed hope for love undying,
violet royal persistence.

Hurry! take the clippers.
Find pretty vases.
Fill your house with
bruises of blossom glow.
Drive the old, tired mining towns
with your windows down.
Breathe.

Swimming The Great Lakes

Even though I knew it from my reading, imagine my gustatory shock the first time I swam in the ocean, in Atlantic City, NJ, the summer I worked there as a waitress. The water was salty!

I.

When I swam in great bodies of water, tossed by white-capped waves, peppered by submerged sand, forced to my knees by the power of the rhythmic shoreline eddies, when the water came into my mouth it was fresh water, for my swimming had been in that geographic core of the Midwest, the Great Lakes—in **Lake Superior**, which is merely barely swimmable in the doldrums of August in the Upper Peninsula of Michigan, when even then the coldness slashes the lungs in a long "oof" and the news is a virus among locals—"Lake Superior is swimmable"--and we all go to our favorite sandy beach nearby; in **Lake Michigan**, north of Chicago, near Fort Sheridan, where I worked as a GS-2 military pay clerk summers during college, and where my co-workers, college students from Wisconsin and Illinois and I had picnics after work on deeply sandy beaches where the water was calmer and warmer than Superior, and then, on the Michigan side, while camping near the majestic Sleeping Bear Dunes or visiting friends in the charming city of Traverse City; in **Lake Erie**, where my kids, husband, and I borrowed his father's 36-foot boat, almost a small yacht, and spent weekends at Put-in-Bay near where Commodore Perry uttered "We have met the enemy and he is ours," navigating among the hordes of tourists seeking the balmy waters and secret beaches only accessible by boat; in **Lake Huron**, at Mackinac Island, where we took a dip with our small, inadequate towels hanging on our rented bikes while peddling around that horseless-carriage-free historic refuge since the 1650s for soldiers and fur traders during the French and Indian War and the War of 1812; in **Lake Ontario**, camping on the way to Niagara Falls in western New York, where a sudden swift undertow began to carry my 9-year-old self out to the larger lake until my gurgles and sinking, gesturing arms led the lifeguard to dive in and save me (I loved swimming so much I went right back in after he delivered me to my scared parents because I didn't want to be too traumatized to swim).

II.

The best swims, though, were in the boreal forest and Precambrian shield rock- encompassed lakes and rivers of my native Midwest place, the Upper Peninsula of Michigan. In this area, many if not most people have second homes or cottages, regionally called "camps," many of them with saunas built in imitation of their ancestors in Finland. The swimming after sauna is the most refreshing of all. We would "steam up" in the sauna, pouring *"loylä"* (cool water with a tinge of sacredness) on the heated rocks, which would sizzle with clouds that would billow up to us sitting naked or in bathing suits on the tiered wooden benches--and when we couldn't stand our beating hearts and sweating hot bodies anymore, we would hurry out jogging down the path, and jump into the lake with a rewarding shout and a "whoosh" of relief; as kids we would do this over and over; as adults, we would wait, chatting in our lawn chairs or across the picnic table, until the kids had had their two or so hours of fun; then we would refill the sauna stove with wood, leisurely sweat up, and take only two or three trips from the sauna to the lake, the last one perhaps with an added-on slow crawl to the middle or across.

As neighborhood children in Ishpeming's Cleveland Location, on the last day of school in June, we would hike through rocky outcrops, birch stands, and cedar swamps a mile or so to Cedar Lake, one of the 7 or so lakes within the city limits of my small (population 8,500 at that time, now 6,000) hometown of Ishpeming (among them Lakes Angeline, Teal, Bancroft, Sally, Deer, Cedar) to baptize ourselves for summer, our fingers side-blinding our eyes like draft horses to ("don't peek!") as we passed the end portion of the lake, called Rocky, where the boys swam naked (as they did in the high school pool), trudging uphill and down to where the girls would swim, at a location on the lake called Shallow. We would walk there, in good weather, several times a week. These glacier-carved lakes dot Upper Michigan, Wisconsin, and Minnesota, and swimming in their sometimes brown tannic but more often translucent clear waters is a northern ritual.

We were good swimmers--better, I have noticed, than many; first, because of the abundance of lakes and rivers in which to swim during our elementary school childhood years, and second, because Ishpeming High School, subsidized by the regional paternalistic Cleveland Cliffs iron mining company, had a pool where we had single-sex lessons once a week for four years, emerging as junior Red Cross lifesavers, knowing the ins and outs of kicks –flutter, frog--and matching strokes—crawl, back, breast, side. We even learned to dive. (Three steps, bounce, and off!) Even today, at 80, I swim as often as I can.

ROBERT POLZIN

Be Aware

Blood for the line god
and skulls for the market throne,
throw corpses under its slope
as you grasp and grope
to sit astride its peak.

Do not be deceived.
You are not the rider.
You do not hold the reins.
The leash is attached to *you*
and the Beast is in the lead.

Sooner or later the algorithmic
mechanism of optimization
will learn how to wring blood
from a stone.

But long before then,
the quiet vines of growth
will coil 'round your gilded fingers
and digital wrists.

The pearls 'round your neck
and the belt 'round your waist
will squeeze and pop you, too,
just like a grape.

And the sweet wine will be enjoyed
purely for its abstract value.

Chute 13

My mother often told me,
"Tread not the harbor after dark.
Though the moon be bright and air so sweet,
there are others who use that park.

"For high above, in the dock of ore,
lurks an awful, fearsome thing
that pines each night for its escape
and so makes the dead rails sing.

"No, I'll not say more, my boy;
there are things better not to know.
Quell, for once, your inquisition;
hear and heed me: do not go!

"And if, forbid, you disobey,
and wander careless on the green,
promise at least, my reckless son,
you'll not gaze upon chute 13!"

Yet I was foolish, reckless too,
and curious to dire fault;
so I resolved, within my heart,
to learn the secret of that swinging vault.

Deep in May in the midnight air,
the scent of lilac on the wind,
I waited in the spruce boughs
of the harbor for it to begin.

The moon hung low as the sky went still
and a groan below hearing began,
then spoke, with the voice of rail cars,
the words of children not of man.

Still I hear their iron calls,
"Please, we want to play!
It gets so lonely in the dark,
but we cannot bear the day.

"It sure is swell to have you here,
strangers so seldom come.
But here you are; it's true! It's real!
Now we can have some fun!"

Bewildered then, my soft reply,
"Come out then, O newfound friends.
The moon is bright, yet I see you not;
if wish you to play: your cloak suspend!"

"Ohhh. . ." they cooed, a slowing train,
"we would, and yet can not.
We're stuck down here, within the chute,
and here forever rot.

"Unless! Oh mister, you could help?
Come free us for a night?
Then we could play, in truth! For real!
We'd dance and scream delight!

"Go up downtown, walk down the tracks,
you'll soon see what we mean.
It's not far, we swear, we've done it before
and we all reached chute 13."

How queer it was that my legs did move
although I bade them stop.
And before control had I regained,
found myself on the ore dock's top!

Despite the fear within my breast
I stood rooted and heard them sing:
"O yea! O yes! You're so very close.
Almost, just one more thing!

"Come closer, now, a handful of steps
and we'll finally be able to start."
But I stood my ground before the chute,
as grim sickness gripped my heart.

"What ask you, ghosts, that I can give?"
I called out to the steel and the black,
the lake air chilled the sweat on my neck,
then I heard them answer back,

"Intrepid souls were we, as you!
Yet now we languish so alone,
for we cannot escape this place
so long as it holds our bones.

"We ask you then, just get them out!
Cast them into the lake.
From there we'll drift to everywhere
and our thirst will at last be slaked."

I felt for them, so trapped down there,
and yet, I answered, "No!
I'm sorry for your plight, my friends,
but I'm afraid that I must go!"

Growled then, the track 'neath my feet,
"If you will not let us roam,"
screeched calamity, the screaming steel,
"you'll join us in our home!"

Poor, lost souls, as red as the rust
came writhing out the chute!
They flung themselves with all abandon
and reached forthwith for my boots!

Their limbs were long and tipped with claws–
no! Fingers worn to the bone
from scraping, clawing against their fate,
ground down by steel and stone.

Their eyes were pellets aglow with rage
and their cries, cacophonous pain.
I turned myself with utmost haste
and ran from that unholy fane.

Though their voices followed with me;
indeed, they haunt me to this day,
their bodies did stop behind me,
as if something blocked their way.

The tracks to the dock have long been cut,
as well the ramp was all torn down.
I do believe that this was best
for the safety of the town.

Though I pity those I met that night,
and for their captured souls, I pray,
I urge you with utmost gravity:
visit the Harbor only in the day.

JANEEN PERGRIN RASTALL

Fossil Hunting at the Quarry

after Gerard Manley Hopkins

Leaves slick our boot bottoms,
you grab my hand. I clutch
a sack. We wind down
the rock cut where
gypsum was pried
from the sediment. We search
for fern fronds impressed
in the chert. Our eyes intent
on patterns in variegated stone,
we never see
the breeze unleaf the birch tree,
gold tumble
to the quarry's heart,
a leaf filigree sink below.

(First published in *The World is Charged: Poetic Engagements with Gerard Manley Hopkins.*)

How to Build a Sauna

How shall we hew the sun. Split it and make blocks - Wallace Stevens

With titanium pick axes, we chip
the sun, hack a chunk off
every dawn. Trees shudder
and surrender their leaves.
Frost licks the lawn with a coated tongue.

We shutter the blinds and stack
our blocks by the furnace.
Steam climbs the basement stairs.
We slam the door
before the neighbors guess
who brings this early winter on.

Learning the Alphabet

Find a rock at Little Presque,
sandstone flecked with copper.
Put it on your tongue.
Sand, grit, bits of bark may slough off.
Roll the rock around.
Mingled with the limonite, the iron,
catch a hint of freighter grease.
Taste salmon and lake trout.
Ore dust may drift back in your throat
and dashes of wintergreen,
tangs of cedar or spring moss.
Slide the stone across the roof of your mouth.
Sip frost on mittens,
wet fur and musk.
Curl your tongue.
Lick the rock like the first icicle
that broke inside your glove.
Suck snowflakes
light on your tongue
and clumps dug
from the base of a ten-foot drift.
When the rock is thinner than a priest's wafer
swallow Superior clear and deep.
Open your lips.
Start with the alphabet.
Say "eh."

(An earlier version first appeared *Border Crossing.*)

Suddenly Falling

Winter had come while they lay together– Tomas Tranströmer

First, frost etches a privacy screen
across the front door pane. Next,
webs of ice seal the mailbox
shut, stitch the newspaper
to frozen grass. Flurries
cling to the window screens.
The wind throws a spread of drifts
over the lawn mower, the rake,
the bag of leaves. While they dream
the pickup's bed collects the snow.

(First published in *Heart Radicals* [About Editions, 2018].)

What the Blizzard Left

Death notices flurry –
a whiteout of altar linens
and quilted casket linings.

We polish our best black shoes
and chart our fragility.
I see the thinness
beneath your ring.
You spy my slow rise
from the chair.

We wander out to see
what the blizzard left—
only white bruising white.

Where is the upturned wheelbarrow,
the half-stacked
cord, the axe imbedded
in a blighted box elder?

Our path from the back
porch is buried. The tops
of pine trees pierce
our soles as we wade
through these drifts.

What the wind once whispered
to autumn leaves
roars in our ears.

Fruit

You can't go into the grocery store and pick one out,
can't hold it in your hand,
its round bottom fitting your palm,
can't check for flaws,
(soft spots that will make the whole section go bad),
put it in a bag
and take it home.

You have to wait.
Sometimes for seasons,
pouring water on a barren tree.

You wander through a neighbor's orchard,
eat some fallen fruit,
save the seeds.

It is about the pruning,
cutting away
even full branches.

In April, you seduce bees.

When a branch begins to droop,
you clamber up.
You reach behind the leaf curtain
and pluck a piece from your tree.

RICHARD J. RASTALL

Know That

for David & Thomas

Know that I love you, because I do.
Know that you are a good person, because you are.
Know that you can do almost anything if you try, practice, work hard and don't quit,
because you can.
Know that you can decide, you can say no,
because otherwise it's not your decision.
Know that you can compare yourself only with yourself, because there is no one like you.
Know yourself and be honest with yourself,
because that is the source of your self-worth.
Know that you will make mistakes, because we all do.
Know that the important things in life are your health, your family and your friends,
because they are.
Know that you are never alone, because you aren't.
Know that there is life after death, because there is.

The Bridge Builder

for Dad

"I had little effect on their lives", he said,
as if the moon's orbit lacked influence on oceans, poets or imagination.
Every other weekend he connected us.
We watched time bob
on surfaces of rivers and streams,
next to our thrown sticks.
We ran from side to side,
tossed stones, laughed,
and explored the banks.
His gaze went beyond the bend,
as he designed spans
upon which I walk today.

(This poem first appeared in *Sing Then I Must*; Poetry Society of Michigan.)

CHERRY PITS

for Mom

Cherry pits roll off a conveyer belt at a rate of about 100 pits per second
and fall 50 feet onto a giant inverted pit-cone.
Encouraged by my mother, I would stand in the center of the stream,
Pits with bits of pulp plummeted on my head leaving cherry stains on my scalp and clothes.
Each second, passing through the pits and my skull were 65 billion solar neutrinos leaving no visible trace.

While a secretary in New York City, my mother and Einstein met at a time when the neutrino had not been detected, only postulated as a zero-mass speed of light particle that could pass through any matter.

Now, we know neutrinos exist and have slightly greater than zero mass, traveling just less than the speed of light. A person can't hide from solar neutrinos on the dark side of the earth, substantially all of them pass through the planet unchanged. Then there are neutrinos passing through, from other universal events, even perhaps a couple from the big bang.

Just how solid are we?

We asked my Mom about her Einstein meeting. At that time, Einstein was trying to solve unified field theory. Incorporating gravity into the theory was always a problem.

The simple force that causes the cherry pit to fall wanted to remain mysteriously aloof from mathematical inclusion, yet, that force is what formed the atoms in stars, caused galaxies to reform around dark holes as spirals from exploded star parts.

Einstein did not know that 7 more dimensions might be needed for unification and that perhaps the slight force of gravity we could measure, leaked from those dimensions. Had he succeeded, unified field theory may have explained what happens to a head simultaneously experiencing 100 cherry pits and 65 billion solar neutrinos in 11 dimension space.

We were in awe of Einstein, and so by proxy, our mother. Periodically, we would pump her with Einstein questions. Would new answers result? Would she remember something more? Or had their meeting left behind no tangible fact of Einstein for us to hold.

Remember, she would say with a gleam in her eye: "Einstein wasn't born in a day. "

(This poem first appeared in *Ice Volcanoes* by Richard J. Rastall, Gordon Publications (2012).)

A Poem Too Good To Be Framed

The poem started from your mind,
lingered in a frame,
until it escaped and embraced me,
and we danced,
and with each twirl there was another image.

(This poem first appeared in *Ice Volcanoes* by Richard J. Rastall, Gordon Publications (2012).)

The Rainbow Tree

We played each summer where the water and sand held hands.
The forest opened at Lost Lake to frogs, herons and sun baked turtles on logs.
From Green Grass Hill we spied people and deer.
The world became a blur loping, then tumbling down the Big Dune.

In that place a solitary tree anchored rainbows.
Our dreams were shattered when we returned dragging home our shovels and empty bucket;
caked sand on our sweaty skin.

Twenty five years later, three generations gather with children
happily playing on the Big Dune under a cloudless blue sky
with the sun's reflection off Lake Michigan on our faces,
at rainbows' end.

(This poem first appeared in the Lansing Poetry Club, *Sixtieth Anniversary Edition*, 1998.)

ICE VOLCANOES

Words ride Lake Superior spray to the shore,
Some stay, some recede,
They twirl in eddies, gasp with the undertow,
Some grab the sand, then the ice,
Some words lack the strength to last,

This process creates shapes, and with time, ice volcanoes.

Ice volcanoes are wonders to experience.

From afar, on rough days, they speak,
with cryo-magma explosions into the sky.

And on quiet days, the curious venture to the cornice, peer down the blue ice,

see the infrastructure reflecting levels and degrees of light.

(This poem first appeared in *Ice Volcanoes 3rd Edition* by Richard J. Rastall, Gordon Publications (2016).)

HELEN HASKELL REMIEN

For My Grandchildren

You will never be alone
that's what I want to tell you
even when you wake up in the middle of the night
and your fairy light is broken
and your room is really dark
Not even then
Not even out in the middle of the huge cedar
and ponderosa forest on the hilly trail
when your mom and dad have marched ahead
or lagged behind, not even when you feel shy
on the playground and the bigger kids are swinging
from monkey bar to monkey bar and you can't
even reach those rungs and you don't know
the names of the big kids and are afraid
they might laugh at you for being small
Not even when the alone feeling is as huge
as the nighttime sky and you are afraid
it might go on forever
Not even then
you will never be alone
and if you stay still for just a moment
breathe deep into your belly's bottom
and out again with a whoosh
you will hear something in that no-wiggle
place of aloneness
You will hear your own breath
will feel something too
your own wiggly toes
your own sturdy legs
your own beautiful body lit up from the inside
and you will remember you are always
here for yourself
and you, dear one, are your own best friend.

This Girl's on Fire

lit up with flames
not measly campfire flames
the kind we had in girl scout overnights
the kind you sit around and tell a good story.
I'm talking bonfire
low tide beach fire, fueled with fallen branches
piles of scruffy brush bleached tree trunks
old rubber sneaker soles
a fire with flames that shoot skyward
sparks that dance with stars
a fire that can hold it all
that burns away everything unwanted
that leaves the woods brush free
the beach clear of debris
the cottage empty of trash
the kind of fire that brings a girl alive
no burning at the stake
no residual welts and swells
the kind of fire that liberates exhilarates
the kind of fire that is washed away
by the incoming tide
that leaves nothing in its wake
no charred wood, no melted sneaker sole
nothing but smooth sand and an ocean
of possibility.

In My Pocket

When he was little, my son carried Boom Boom
in the pocket of his Oshkosh overalls.
Boom Boom was an imaginary pig who could fit
in the tiniest of places. My son would hold him in his outstretched
pre-school-sized hand, introduce him to strangers.
"This is Boom Boom," he would say.
Boom Boom traveled with us to Florida on a plane, to Maine
in the cupholder of a car seat, to bed each night,
his head resting on the pillow next to my sons.
My toddler son was tender with Boom Boom, careful
not to crush him, a loyal friend to his tiny pig.

Death, I have not always been as gentle with you.
I shove you in the pocket of my down-filled jacket along
with the crystal and a dog treat and sometimes
forget you are even there.
I zip you away, don't want anything to do with you.
But I think you would like Boom Boom.
He tells funny jokes, makes toddlers laugh.
Tomorrow, on my walk, when I grasp the crystal,
I will reach in for you, pull you out as gently
as my son reached for his tiny pig and I'll let you
ride on my shoulder, and I will share with you the budding aspen,
the blossoming arbutus.
I will pick one white blossom,
hold it under your nose, let you smell how good it is to be alive
in the Northwoods on a sunny day in May.

This Love

for Cam on our 44th Wedding Anniversary

does not follow a recipe
though cookbooks line the kitchen shelf.
This love is no longer gourmet sauces that require
heavy cream, lots of stirring, hours and hours of fussing,
no longer fourteen courses, a souffle and a baked Alaska,
No this love has gotten easier with time.
It is chopped garlic, a shallot flung into a forty year old
Le Creuset pan, a quick sauté and some chopped greens
because this love might be as old as the pan, but it is
farm fresh, local, organic, spinach, bok choy, sometimes
the excitement of asparagus.
This love is pasta shaped like bowties,
a splash of the exotic, virgin olive oil from the Greek island where Aphrodite resides.
This love is peppery, the lick of salt on fingers,
a sprinkle of asiago because cheese adds breadth.
It is a ripe strawberry, an August peach still warm
with sun, a honey crisp bite of apple.
This love is sometimes bitter, dandelion greens, dark chocolate
because bitter is okay,
can be tempered with a sweet onion, a spoonful of honey

From Somewhere to Somewhere Else.

I can't remember where we were going
or where we had been.
Perhaps we had visited our very old mother along the coast
and I, the little sister, was driving you back to Connecticut
in my rental. It is hazy now over a decade later,
though I do remember the day was summery bright
and we were coasting along the back roads of Maine.
You insisted we stop at Dunkin Doughnuts
because their coffee is the best.
And we spoke of our husbands, your pottery, my yoga
and you shared your dream with me.
I remember that clearly, how you wanted to move
back to Maine after retirement, buy an old farmhouse,
set up a pottery studio, open a bed & breakfast.
Your husband would do the handiwork;
you'd turn your pots, bake muffins for the guests.
I, your little sister, was your cheerleader, your coach.
You, my big sister, who had taught me to sew,
who had designed my wedding dress,
lined it with silky fabric, crocheted the buttonholes,
allowed me to help you design your dream that day.
And together, stitch by stitch, we pieced it into place
and it didn't matter whether you slipped it on
at some later date, because while meandering
from somewhere to somewhere else,
you had already moved in, had set your pots for sale,
and we two sisters were sitting at the long pine table
in your kitchen, filling ourselves up with muffins,
freshly baked.

BERT RIESTERER

(1935-2018)

Donnelly Wilderness Preserve

Nestled in a huge gorge,
the river peacefully uncoils its way
to the distant lake.

Intermittent sunshine casts
a blinding gleam on select stretches.

Stone based wavelets mimic
the twists of wary trout.

High above its broad banks
I wander the tree rich trail.
Ancient hemlocks, spruce, pine
and cedar reign majestically,
unabashed by the occasional
challenge of feisty young saplings.

Total quiet, blessed peace.

The soul supplants the self.

Boundaries fade.

The rarity of Oneness.

Softly

Softly
Silently
Soothingly
Snow
Spreads
Serenity
Over my
Stubborn
Stolid
Soul

Morning

From afar, tight-fisted dawn
moves silently through the night.

Finally at the horizon
she opens her palms,
carefully smearing clutched rosy
hues among indifferent clouds.

The wind yawns, stretches gently,
fluffing awakening tree tops.

A ragged flock of impatient
geese honk a brief greeting.

Street lights loath to turn off
sulk in the growing light.

School buses rumble past.
My coffee needs rewarming.
Good morning, Marquette.

Writer's Block

[I'm bombarded with poems
but finding the words to explode
or defuse them is a helluva task]

Steelhead

Bent round,
it lay like a
damp rag discarded
at the river's mouth.

Its jaw slightly open,
the eye still glaring defiance
despite death's clamp.

Behind the head
above the lateral,
it was torn open
and thoroughly purged
of juicy, savory, muscle and flesh.

The curved spine untouched
as were fins and tail.

The cold hard sheen of the
intact head was irresistible.
My heel confirmed the name.

CHRISTINE SAARI

Sentinels

Three are left behind the house,
three conifers, tall and tattered.
My father planted them at his mountain farm
when he began his new life before the War.
Planted rows of trees to form a rectangle,
named it *Tanneneck,* German for square of firs.

They grew tall and taller over eighty years,
spread their branches, dropped their cones,
served as playground for squirrels. Crows spied from their tops.
They fell one by one, in storms racing up the mountain,
struck by lightning, cut to give each other room.

Today only three are left, in vigil over the valley.
When I stand on surrounding hills,
I search for these sentinels to find the farm,
see them reach into the sky from far away,
telling me, there is my home.

I trust, they will outlive me,
tower over the red tile roof for years to come,
guide our sons and grandchildren
when they hike, run in the hills,
search for the farm in the distance.

The Dollhouse

Day after day I sat
and worked at the dollhouse.
While towers burst into flames,
I laid wooden floors in tiny rooms.
While people jumped out of windows,
I placed tile after tile on the steep roof.
While New Yorkers ran dazed through the streets,
I made shutters and windows and doors.
While families searched for their loved ones,
I painted and hammered and sawed.

I thought of my granddaughter Lily,
four years old, and the changed world,
she would live in from now on.
I thought of Vicek, the young Pole,
forced laborer on our Austrian farm.

In the midst of a war, at Christmas 1944,
he built a dollhouse for me,
the four-year-old daughter of his enemies.
I thought of the healing work of hands,
of creating beauty in the face of destruction.

By Christmas the house was finished.
I scoured junk shops and thrift stores.
I found an iron cooking stove, tables and chairs.
I found beds and couches and chests.
I found a cradle, a highchair, a bassinet
I found dishes of pewter, enamel, ceramic,
a tin colander from my own childhood.
I found miniature dolls to live in the house:
Father, mother, a boy, a girl and a baby.
Their furniture was eclectic as our own.

Lily plays with her dollhouse the minute she
walks in the door, at Christmas, on the Fourth of July.
She creates story after story for her family,
invents drama, adventure and directs their lives.
Her people arrange and re-arrange the furniture.
They clean and they cook and they play.
They lie in their beds and sit on their chairs.
They gleefully discover something new:
A sewing machine or tiny books on a shelf,
a basket, a telephone, a Mongolian pot.

For Lily this house is a place of safety
amid the anxieties and fears of her life.
Here she lives in a world without illness or war.
No evil befalls her people. She controls their fate.
Grown up now and going to college,
she still finds comfort in her miniature world.

Postcards

I sort postcards.
Postcards from a lifetime.
Postcards that criss-crossed the globe.
I sort. My intent is to purge.

Easter wishes from my Vienna friend,
mailed to Western College when I studied abroad.
I wish you were here,
Ilse writes in her elegant script.
Now that she has died
this message seems evermore poignant

Greetings sent from Austria to Taiwan:
a preprinted Chinese address,
gold-rimmed, finely etched stamps
of the Vienna Opera House.
Happy fifth anniversary, my mother says.
A year ago, the Russians occupied Prague...

My mother's card from Israel
to her two-year old grandson in Boston.
Imagine, I am now
where the Christ Child was born!
The image: two little boys riding a mule. A mule,
like the one my father once promised to bring home.

Four colorful peasant girls
in their cave home, stitching.
A postcard to our sons and their father
from my solo trip to China.
I felt pangs of guilt for deserting my family.
At the same time, I relished my freedom.

Postcards from friends who married
and had children, who traveled the world.
From relatives, aghast we planned a China year.
Who will pay for that? wonders my aunt.
When are you coming home?
my mother pleads.

Each card contains a whole world.
The sender has chosen an image -
a Madonna, a flower, a landscape,
has sent a message written by hand.
Colorful stamps tell about the course of history
from postwar Austria to the European Union.

Addresses retrace my life:
The town house of my High School days,
student rooms in Vienna, Graz, Oxford Ohio.
Stays abroad in England and America,
apartments during early marriage,
our first house where we still live.

There are wishes for special occasions,
precious glimpses of simple daily life:
My mother's delight over her garden,
a friend's joy when her grandchild laughs,
a grandson's drawing of a spider,
words of longing, of waiting for mail.

It seems no one writes postcards today.
How can I throw out these treasures!
Three shoeboxes take up little space.
I put them back into my closet
next to bundles of letters, clipped articles,
old photographs.

Darning Socks

These socks, red and blue striped,
made just for me, warmed my feet
on my icy walk around Presque Isle.
When I take them off, each has a hole.

My friend Ilse from Vienna knit them,
for Christmas. She loved sending
her hand-made gifts. Greeting cards,
embroidered pillows, woolen socks.

Now no more socks will come from Ilse.
I must to mend them. No better time
to darn than this day, when schools, businesses
are closed, when everyone is holed up inside.

I find the fat darning needle, stuck in a lace pin cushion.
From the porch I retrieve the basket of mending wool.
I spy a bright red ball, just what I need,
grateful there are no signs of moths.

I sew a circle around the hole,
make a tight grid of threads,
length-wise and sideways. I sew in and out,
until a firm criss-cross pattern closes the gap.

When I was eight, my mother's friend Christi
taught me how to mend. From then on I repaired
our torn woolens, prolonged their life in post-war Austria.
My mother too impatient for this meditative work.

Over the years I have gotten lazy.
Have discarded socks in need of repair.
Not these socks! I want them to last
until it is time for me to join my friend.

Visiting the Uncles in Iron Belt, Wisconsin, 1979

Bouncer and Vern, the uncles, sit at the kitchen table,
arms folded above their bulging bellies.
Beer flows, stories pour out all night.

The story of the cow in the shed behind the house,
a little white company house, number 10, on Main Street
in the town of Montreal, Wisconsin, near the Michigan border.
The cow kept our family alive during depression days,
but later, none of us five siblings wanted to milk it.
When we got rid of it, says Bouncer, we *were not sorry at all.*

The story of Mother, sending Bouncer after Father in the bar.
When he did not return, sending out son number two.
Once he was on a twister of several days, Bouncer recalls.
When he came home, the house was empty. Mother had left.
He had to take the train and retrieve her from a relative's house.
But she did come back.

The story of the death of the father, widowed for sixteen years,
retired from the mine, ill with silicosis.
In the end, he spilled all his blood, says Bouncer.
I held the bucket. So much blood, there was none left in his body.
Yet, his heart beat on for twenty more minutes.
A ghastly death to observe. He was only sixty-four when he died.

Stories of speaking Finn with the elders,
of strikes and labor unions,
of mines closing and people leaving.
Montreal is a ghost town now. Down to 200 people, says Bouncer.
He and Vern, widowed both, stayed,
each in their own house, rarely seeing each other.

Our visit brings them together to tell of a childhood they share.
But Bouncer still interrupts his younger brother
when he tries to tell tales of his own.

REBECCA TAVERNINI

In the Pand

The movies are all old.
The couch with Jerry, George and Elaine.
The Sharknado beach scenes, before we're all devoured.

It's an everything.
It's a before and after.
Demarcation point.
March 2020.
Brandenburg Gate.
9-11.

History is lost, and breeding
on us.

Reset the clock.
It's been 11:58 for days.
Or not.

We dream the same stream:
Carrying hairy cows to safety.
Burying monkeys in couches.

Longing for the electricity,
of your fingertips next to mine.
Not touching mine.

I just want to sleep.
Ask strangers,
"Let me in your dream."

I am seeking a dream.
A cloudbank of near
forgotten scents.

Start this sentence
with me,
unknown, broken soul.

Solar Night

No one sees the lit
pine tree. It glows anyway.
Just in case.

Memos

Late-day light in late December glows blue
beneath my snowshoe imprints, like lily pads on a secret lake
peering through.

Late-month thaw reveals the wide conversational dashes of otters
trespassing the snow, then a hole in the ice, a period,
portal to mollusks below.

The late-arriving jet slices the atmosphere like scissors locked on a wrapping paper's path.
The late decade's penultimate week falls like heavy debts
of snow from weighted branches, sending sound waves through the still air,
ticking nearly imperceptibly.

Late-season blue jays and chickadees command their platoons
with a few chosen tunes threaded like a hem through the treetops.

In last-week's *Times*, my pen interprets acrostics, transcribing knowledge,
or not, on a thin sheet of tree, as if that's enough to transmit
what we know so far.

It's enough.
It's all enough.
The whispering clouds' indelible tracks,
the bubbles rising and bursting from the riverbed,
the vermiculated word search underneath the rock.

Late Mom. Late Dad. Late Friend.
I search for your message prism,
foreign vocalization, shout to the heart from a marching band drum.
Let me peer in there for an instant, while the sound and the light
is vacant.

As the Snow Lays Wool upon its Mat

As the snow lays wool upon its mat,
and the winds fill the sky's skein
of geese leaving,
Spirit seeks a reckoning,
reaches into the tilting pines, slanting sun,
hours unraveling in the fade.
After all, the ruffed grouse flies
into the window pane.
The muskrat is nearly cased in ice.
Coyote travels in one direction.

Where the raspberry thickets scraped
my worthwhile arms,
columbine sang by the gravel,
and in a truck he passed by
without seeing.

Scenes under another winter's detritus.
Walk on tracks, wonder whose,
when they are my own.
Muskrat warns with a splash.
This is different than the past.

Funerals

I bait the spring loaded
mousetrap with one nut,
feed myself another.

Living room. Living room.
Is what Barbara said at the end.
She means the womb,
explained the celibate father.
The womb where we all begin,
and can't imagine a better life.

The last mouse I caught
looked alive, its eyes
brown globes expecting better.

Who would believe a world so beautiful—
oceans, mountains, animals—
a place so unimaginable was waiting
for Barbara? And for us?
He intoned. Swung the incense globe.

I have a Ziploc bag of pine traps
stamped VICTOR with a red V
silhouetted with ears and eyes
where a mouse fits
perfectly between its thighs.

JOHN TAYLOR

Marionettes

The curtains rise on a stage called Now
For a show for children who pretend they
can't see the Marionette's wires making
the all applaud the puppet master's crimes

It goes like this:

A Madman
    Becomes a dictator
    Becomes a god
    Becomes a string

And the Marionettes dance

A Person
    Becomes a follower
    Becomes a warrior
    Becomes a string

And the Marionettes gather

A Lie
    Becomes a rumor
    Becomes the truth
    Becomes a string

And the Marionettes march

A Loss
    Becomes a rally
    Becomes a riot
    Becomes a match

And the Marionettes burn

The curtains fall to a standing ovation
For the mad puppet master's show
It was always about him, not the
Marionettes he played like Nero's
fiddle, never telling them the stage
was their funeral pyre.

Next show's at three

The Damned Monsters

Once we were afraid to look under the bed
Or "They" would get us in the night for sure
The Devil, Krampus, The Slender Man, whoever
Always hiding around the corner or in the closet
Making sure we listened to the grown-ups
Because they only took "the bad kids"

Good kids were safe from the Damned Monsters

We saw our families drown on dry land
In bottles of liquor and pills daily
Saw our priests do the Devil's work
Who could protect us when they got home
When dishes broke and belts came off

When we were alone with the Damned Monsters?

We grew up and painted our eyes black
Listened to Metal, watched horror flicks
Saw our families cross themselves when
we walked into the room with occult books
Utterly aghast at our wicked Goth ways

"How can you like those Damned Monsters?"

What was so bad about monsters, anyway?
All they did was follow their true nature
At least they were honest about killing you
Not hiding behind an insurance denial letter
like the bastard who killed Grandma did

Honorable things, those Damned Monsters...

Now we're afraid to turn on the TV
To see dictators scream about rockets
See more schools become shooting ranges
Thoughts and prayers as churches burn
We sip coffee, paralyzed by the revelation;

We were safer with the Damned Monsters

(Originally published in Liber Dulcis Dolorum: The Book of Sweet Sorrows, in 2021.)

Nighttime in a Snow-globe

In the dark sphere of ice I find solace
the inner peace only snow grant me
the promise of the impending solstice
Gives my soul flight on freezing winds

The snowbound world beacons me tonight
to it's white canvas where dreams are written
in peppermint red wrapped in verdant green
giving life to a child's pure hearted dreams

Beneath the northern skies bright aurora
the pagan and prophetic in one combine
in shining starlight caught in silver bells
and small scarlet orbs of blazing chrome

Wise men exchange gifts beneath Odin's tree
Angels and Valkyrie dance in falling snow
Mistletoe and Frankincense lend sweetness
to crisp night air and Yule logs burning bright

The King of Kings and Queen of Ice
smile at each other in peaceful splendor
Their children rejoice at the truce of
heaven and earth on a starry night

Joy to the world of swirling snow
an ancient hymn the chorus sings
reaching the bright aurora above
the icy boughs of evergreen trees

In the east stars fade in waxing light
of the vibrant dawning solstice sun
a restful halt for a to a joyous revel
peace lingers on the morning winds

On the mantle rests the icy world
an oaken Atlas bears a glassy dome
The snow globe world settles calm
for another cold night's dreaming

The Dinosaur's Horoscope

"Asteroids do not concern me, Admiral..." -Darth Vader, Star Wars Episode V

Was Saturn in retrograde on that hot Cretaceous night?
When the stars fell to Earth and ended the reign of
Of the tyrant lizard king? When stone fell from the sky
Consigning the ruling Sagittarius to a fossilized grave?

Did the Triceratops know that its fight would never end
With the swift footed thieves of their nests? It wasn't in
the cards, The Triceratops was a Taurus after all, but
Velociraptors are Leos and will always have their way

Could the Maiasaurus look to the sky and sing
Twinkle, Twinkle little Star to its young?
That Hadrosaur Pisces, such a good mother
Wishing on the shooting star that doomed her

Did an Amargasaurus know it's solar ascendant?
Did it care about its sun sign as feasted on leaves?
Did it see itself in the constellations shining above?
Did it see its demise flash across the horizon?

I wonder if dinosaurs had prophets among them?
A Nodosaur Nostradamus or Raptor Revelation
To warn them the Apocalypse was coming to
Bring about the a mass extinction yet again?

But there was no Age of Aquarius in the Age
of Dinosaurs, no New Age of mystical rebirth
Just a million megaton Mesozoic blast from
above to ring in the coming of the Ice Age

Did awestruck mammals look up in the ashes
At the night sky that destroyed their reptilian
overlords? Did they seek to divine what the signs
held for them as they wished on shooting stars?

Even the wisest could not tell a Dinosaur's Horoscope
Written in the glow of dead stars beneath Cycad trees
On a hot Cretaceous night when Saturn was in retrograde
And Wormwood was a Tyrannosaur's unlucky star

Old Photos of the Future

Old Photos of the Future, on sale for dirt cheap, going fast!
In a crumpled envelope at a Kansas flea market table
A six year old boy looks at them in rapt fascination
Grandma sees the "Collector's Edition" label, and buys
Her six year old sees a Science Fiction book come true

Old Photos of the Future, Where Armstrong and Aldrin Walk
on the moon and salute a flag, just like Grandma does
They left all their things there in the lunar dust, like
a summer cabin they promised they'd take the kids to
Before they behaved like an adult making a promise

Old Photos of the Future, where a moon buggy looked
so shiny and cool, much newer than our bragging
Neighbor's rusty Oldsmobile, or the taxi we rode there in
But was older than the broken junk of the Reagan era
That buried it on a worn table in the summer sun

Old Photos of the Future that would never come
Like an unsent break up letter to an ex-lover, lost,
Crumpled in an envelope and forgotten until it was
Sold to a Grandma oblivious to the six year old
Who dreamed of walking with them on the night sky

MIRIAM TAYLOR

Angels, Where are You?

I arose early one morning
Angels all around me
Glowing peace, shining love
Guarding me with their shields
While soaring through the golden sky!
Patiently waiting for a cry
Angels high, angels low
Observing my every move

When danger is near-
Angels where are you now?
Are you near, are you far?
Where are you?
I feel all alone in the dark
Stormy night
Soon everything was calm
They are by my side

Taking charge over me
giving me shelter from the storm
peace is here in this heart of mine
And love abides there, too
It shines like a star in the sky
shines boldly from my heart
with radiance and joy
May angels take charge over you

Giving you peace, granting you love
May they guard you, shield you
Keep you safe I pray
But will you open up your heart?
Will you give Him charge over you?
Angels there when you call
To guard, to love, to give you shelter
To help you all the year through

(Originally appeared in "A Declaration of Love" by Miriam Taylor (Black) in 2003, published in the United Kingdom.)

Hidden Treasure

Wandering in the desert
So far away from home
Looking everywhere
for Hidden Treasure
Digging in the sand
But finding nothing

Walking along the river blue
Admiring the tall green trees
The beautiful flowers at my feet
Sparrows twitter gently in my ear
But as for Hidden Treasure
where can it be?

Sitting at the foot of a mountain
staring up at the Sun, Moon, and stars
What an awesome sight!
Gazing about me in peace and harmony
but as for Hidden Treasure
I find nothing

Climbing the highest mountain
Step by step, minute by minute
Time flies by
Still searching for treasure
I manage to reach the top
but the Treasure isn't there

Standing at the mountaintop
I've looked everywhere
I fall to my knees
Discouraged and in tears
Where's that Treasure
I've been searching for?

After a while, all is still and quiet
I hear a small voice saying
"You've looked everywhere
except your own heart"
Within a moment I jump to
my feet, rejoicing

I've found the Hidden Treasure: the love of God down in my heart

(Originally published in "A Declaration of Love" By Miriam Taylor (Black) in 2003 in the United Kingdom.)

A Year of Peace

On Rosh Hashanah it is written
On Yom Kippur it is sealed
On this new year my prayers start
Grant me a good year to come

In perfect harmony with God, my heart cries
Forgive me for the mistakes I made this last year
Inscribe our names lovingly in the Book of Life
Grant me a good year to come

Help me, Adonai, to be wise in your eyes
Lead me, Adonai, in your ways
Be magnified by my lips as I praise Your name
Grant me a good year to come

Let me walk in Your ways and keep your Mitzvot
Let me reach out to others with your love
Adonai, grant me a year of peace, amen
Grant me a good year to come

Perfect Love: a Cinderella Story

Once upon a starlit evening, a lady stood
Dressed in rags with tangled hair
An orphan enslaved by cruel fate
Sweeping the floors of crumbs and
laboring over a hot iron stove

Her heart searching for perfect love

Hearing whispers of a party nearby
"Love to be had," her aching heart cried
Wishing to belong for just one night but
how to escape her wicked stepmother's
clawed grasp that left her dress in tatters

Atop her dreams of perfect love

The step sisters smile as they leave
Mocking the beautiful soul they could
never have, masked by their red shoes
and sparkling dresses, their
shiny earrings, and perfect robes

With no thought of perfect love

The Lady answers the door for a fairy in radiant blue
“Why are you here?” was her shocked cry
“To make your dreams come true,” was the reply
With a wave of the wand she stood in blue, with sparkling nails
and glass slippers perfect for the party and carriage outside

A gift of perfect love

To the party she goes, dancing her heart out
People grow jealous as she falls in love with
the prince until midnight strikes and she disappears
with her dress, leaving a only a crystal shoe behind
life back to normal, heartbroken and sorrowful

Separated from her perfect love

Until her prince was searching the town
“If the shoe fits I'll marry,” he says
At the last house, the shoe finds it's match
“I'm free!” her heart cries as finally she'll
marry her prince that awesome day

And they lived in perfect love

My Hand in Yours

(co-writer John Taylor)

Being married with a disability means The other half
Of your heart can be half of your mind and body, too
Learning your loves' strengths and your weaknesses
Is the key to a world of wonder through grief...

My love, so caring and kind
Who takes the time to learn
My every care and weakness
Strong in my eyes and
The love of my life

Beloved, so tender and mild
Who showed me your every strength
Discovered my scars unflinchingly
Teaching an iron heart to love

The princess rescues the knight

Walking life's path hand in hand
Bearing in mind where strengths lie
Helping each other when we fall
Teaching each other the way of God
Walking in the light of His love

Life's path is grim and treacherous
We'll face it ever together, beloved
Raising each other ever higher as we
Cross the Valley of the Shadow of Death

The princess rescues the knight

Love is a thing that is built as much as is felt
Working as a team, that builds a strong relationship.
The Strongest tool in your hand is always another hand
The Path may be rocky, but it's all about the hand we hold…

RUSSELL THORBURN

Cold Snap

I wonder why cold has to snap; fingers
can barely move when frozen, hoping to unlock
the getaway car from the tundra of a parking lot.
Temperature signs advertise our downfall:
five degrees below zero. I imagine the whole world
sinking like the Bismarck into frigid Atlantic waves.
My favorite film as a ten year old, slouching
in sticky seats where a barrage of small candy objects
proved deadly to cyclopean eyes too wide.
All those pre-teens in a throwing frenzy.
Our only radar system was to duck as we settled
settled down to watch. Death proved too interesting
to ignore; the British commander in his determined remark
said those famous words, "We must sink the Bismarck."
We didn't want the Bismarck to sink.
That super fortress blew the guts from British cruisers;
an uneasy stillness stuck to us, like the cold
in my later years. I won't mention my age
or where I am watching the time and thermometer,
except it's at McDonald's and I have no job.
They price the coffee at the current temperature
when it falls so far. They owe me many nickels
for this week of the Arctic chill. Walking around,
we have no idea when the cold will unsnap,
like some rubber band at the other end of winter.
I stare at slow-moving vehicles covered in permafrost.
Then snap my fingers. Just like that, I am unemployed,
and my wife tells me to leave the house. She says nothing
of this feeling of helplessness. Work is a dream chariot,
and you wait for a job that never comes; back at home,
faucets leaking keep up this steady beat against porcelain.
But I sit here with a pencil, a pad of paper; I know
how to write, turning around on a page that's eating
words: coffee drunk like wine, never enough: putting
everything in order, even this snap; the burning cold
of us seated at a table, looking at our watches
like finding Hiroshima in their radium glow
before we say suddenly it's time to go.

Electric Garage

At my grandmother's piano in the den,
all of the player rolls in boxes stripped off the top,
the treadles no longer pumped by feet
to drive a song around without touching
the keys, I sat losing myself in chords
seated before the faded smile of ivory,
yellowish with chip-toothed ebony,
and wondered if I would ever be in a real band.
I made a path for us by stacking piano parts
to my friend John's deeply struck guitar.
He traded his Les Paul for an acoustic,
after the garage band days fizzled,
and the bass player crashed his motorcycle
the same year Duane Allman in a deadly spin
on his Triumph ended his life in Macon,
that Fender bass of my friend never played again.
Our electric garage days over, we had no future
but still practiced rock and roll in the den,
without the drummer who snapped his snares
like breaking bones. Our noise attracted
student nurses from next door to our window.
They requested the name of our band. I mumbled Henry.
I peered into the eyes of a blue-eyed shiny nurse,
who didn't care about us that much anyway,
or why I had named our band after my great-grandfather,
who had come from Switzerland to live in Detroit.
The jangling guitar John breathed into his vocals
to match something about so many boys
on the nightly news coming home in body bags;
and me wearing tee shirts, unshaven for the most part,
long hair, pitched my tent at the piano,
until one day I sold it for a hundred dollars,
threw in a banjo, and hitchhiked north.

My Dreams Never Caught Their Bus

I looked into the mirror and a feather treatment
had brushed away my youth. I saw an older man
staring back in the image of Captain Beefheart
when he played at a ballroom in Detroit
and walked onstage before the Kinks
wearing his crushed hello of a hat down over ears.
I was younger then without those under-eye
veins and mottled nose, hairs riding
the dirty shells of my ears; and dreams were shot
with quick camera work for a young man

in his twenties trying to wake up
before it was late afternoon—and that pillow
where my younger self lay became a drug
to forget the draft I was avoiding.
The silence in the house like a museum
for my last days on earth. But that never came despite
my trying; dreams burned like Viking boats
out in a mysterious harbor somewhere,
and the war crept closer on television,
while the curly dark tangled hair of a woman
on shore beckoned before the dream channel
changed to missing the Woodward Avenue bus
in the rain. That's exactly what I did,
running too late for the bus downtown.
I was older than yesterday. These dreams
never caught their bus and left me standing in the rain,
unable to find that right break in becoming a poet;
those busted mattresses with their springs like hairy
armpits showing and crows circling in applause
for such a performance, if only crows had
ice cream, what Captain Beefheart wished
in the Mojave Desert bursting with those
words in an MTV video that was never shown
for being too weird. I barefooted it
to the bathroom, an old man now, my ritual late
this morning staring at those veins declaring
there was Captain Beefheart in the mirror.
I had never given him any thought until
that loss of hair and a bolder brow
was accidentally broken apart by radar
detecting an assault from a foreign country
and that was middle age, beyond that even,
as I mused over his verbose mustache excited
being below his nose and joined to that movable
upper lip, for he had crept into my life
and when he would leave was never discussed,
bringing up my hands to drown that face in my fingertips.

In a Ghostly Cat Glow of Green Christmas Tree Lights

The late movie glows in the green
from the large console losing control horizontally.
A seven-year-old boy occupies floor space
near the saddle-shoed feet of a great aunt
wearing blue fur like an ancient cat,
but is unable to slink away on unsteady legs
to her rapt contemplation of the world.
There are powder puffs and jars in my mother's room,
her lonely temple where she keeps a much younger face,
and her hair is black in old photographs.
Detroit was where we picked up my grandmother
as a hostage on Christmas Eve, and I had to bide
my time before anyone decided the night
of cigarettes and smoky reverie was complete.
In the cramped kitchen with a small table,
not large enough for anything but to sit and drink,
my mother holds her highball. I am a stranger
all dressed up for the evening, a glance at this boy
she barely recognizes, a turn of her delicate Welsh
face with the arching Roman nose of her kin—
and it's this beautiful woman in a dress she sewed
herself that startles me, her slender figure of a sophisticate,
who's letting herself go among the wild animals
of her husband's relatives. Each lit cigarette expels
more smoke; desperate to leave, I pull on my mother's arm:
escape is sleep, and tomorrow morning will come
when I wake up or don't see my father escorting
grandmother to his car. His pork pie hat tipped to one side,
a parrot's green feather stuck in its rim and his freshly shaved
skin glistening in the night's glow. My grandmother
kisses anyone who moves into view; her warm body
wearing a squirrel fur I will have to sit next to
in the long car ride home from Detroit.

Marilyn's Busty as Ever in her Jean Jacket on Location for the Making of *The Misfits*

Pyramid Lake, Nevada, 1960

The cowboy's dog, Dooley, restless
on his leash, bites the hand
of Marilyn who attempted to feed it
a morsel, smelling animals about to die.
Hawks circle above in a cloudless sky
over their flatbed's shadow;
and cowboys too old for Hollywood
see ghosts drift off the mountains
like the end of their careers.
Her character Roslyn won't know
the mustangs are for pet food at first,
not pets for children, as the cowboys
jabber to dismiss their before-scene jitters.
She stands alone in the world,
the boom finally holding out its ear
over fine dust, her eyes flashing
she missed her chance in loving;
her white hair across her brow
like some confession when a photographer
catches her before the shot
dense with hot blood.
And if she could go home she would,
but first her tits must shout to the mountains:
the world is taken by surprise
every time she falls.

Appreciation

Thank you to Matt Maki, Claudia Drosen and Janeen Pergrin Rastall for your efforts in starting the Marquette Poets Circle and to establish the monthly work shop and open mic. Thank you to the Peter White Public Library for hosting the monthly work shop and open mic.

Thank you to all the contributors who submitted for this anthology. Thank you for your assistance with this publication.

Thank you to Janeen Pergrin Rastall for countless suggestions and assistance during the editing process.

Contributors

GIDEON ACHATZ

Gideon Achatz is an eighth grader from Aspen Ridge Middle School. He plans to become a U. S. Poet Laureate and a Nobel Prize-winning writer when he grows up. He also wants to be a primatologist.

MARTIN ACHATZ

Martin Achatz is the Adult Programming Coordinator at Peter White Public Library and a Contingent Professor in the English Department at Northern Michigan University. He served two terms as U. P. Poet Laurate. His book of poems, *The Mysteries of the Rosary*, was published by Mayapple Press. He has released two spoken-word albums, *Slow Dancing with Bigfoot* and *Christmas with Bigfoot*. His most recent work can be read on his blog, *Saint Marty*, at saintmarty-marty.blogspot.com.

ERIN ANDERSON

Erin Anderson first came to Michigan's Upper Peninsula in 1990 from Southern California. During the following twenty years, she left nine times to teach English in Eastern Europe, Central Asia, the Middle East, and the Caucasus, but the UP has remained the only place she wants to live while in the US. She has graduate degrees in English from California State University, Northridge, and Northern Michigan University. She also has an MA in Teaching English to Speakers of Other Languages from the School for International Training. She has written over thirty travel articles for *Relax Magazine* (Ventura County, California) and over twenty personal essays for The Porcupine Press. Her literary essays have appeared *in Bending Genres, Cream City Review, Mississippi Review, Old Northwest Review, Oxford Magazine, Palo Alto Review, Slow Trains, The Square Table, Summerset Review, The Thaw, Windhover, and Word Riot.*

ESTHER MARGARET AYERS

Esther Margaret Ayers lives and works in Marquette, Michigan as a writer, piano teacher and accompanist. She studied at the Yeats International Summer School in Sligo, Ireland, and holds a BME in music and an MA in English, both from Northern Michigan University.

E.M. BARRY

E.M. Barry (Marie Barry) is a Marquette native, having lived here most of her life, except for various sojourns into the outer world following her military husband to far away places with strange sounding names. She has always enjoyed writing.....whether poetry, short stories or journaling. Writing is how she make sense of her life! She is also an avid knitter, reader, and love hiking and being in the woods. Now she lives and writes happily here in the U.P. with a cat named Zelda, lots of yarn, and too many books (if there is such a thing)!

MILTON J. BATES

Milton J. Bates is the author of books about Wallace Stevens, the Vietnam War, and the Bark River watershed in Wisconsin. His poetry includes the collection *Stand Still in the Light* (2019) and two chapbooks, *Always on Fire* (2016) and *As They Were* (2018). He lives in Marquette, where he received the city's Art Award for writing in 2020.

A. LYNN BLUMER

A. Lynn Blumer lives in Marquette, MI where she enjoys the north and being involved in her local art and poetry scene. She works with two non-profits, does odd jobs for monetary ends, and spends her free time writing and printing zines as *Pyre Publishing.* Her personal work has appeared in *Maiden Voyage* by *Gordon Publications, Horror Sleeze Trash: Poems* and their anthology *Prose in Poor Taste, Paper and Ink Literary Zine: Rebellion,* as well as online with *Cephalo Press.* Her first chapbook, *Wayward Creatures*, was released by *Between Shadows Press.* You can follow her on Instagram @pyre_publishing or on GoodReads as herself.

TERRI BOCKLUND

Terri Bocklund is a relative newcomer to Michigan's Upper Peninsula, with deep family roots in the region. Growing up in the Twin City suburbs, she enjoyed writing songs, poetry, and stories. While lyrics for her original songs have been her main poetic efforts in the past, she has recently focused more on poems that do not serve as lyrics, and are not to be bound to musical content. Terri was an Artist in Residence at Isle Royale National Park as a songwriter and composer, and has a suite of music that was inspired by that experience.

FIONA BYRNE-RYAN

Born and raised in Dublin, Ireland, Fiona moved to Detroit in 2016. In October 2021 Fiona and her family made the conscious decision to start living in their truth. Trading in the house for the tent, cement for the dirt, and societal rules to live wild and free. Creating a project called Running Into a New Earth, the couple ran 227 miles of the North Country Trail to raise money and awareness for the Stop Line 3 Resistance. Fiona and her family are currently winter camping in Marquette County while running their online community Truthfully Living.

LYNN DOMINA

Lynn Domina is the author of two collections of poetry, *Corporal Works* and *Framed in Silence,* and the editor of a collection of essays, *Poets on the Psalms.* Her most recent book is *Devotions from HERstory: 31 Days with Women of Faith.* She teaches English at Northern Michigan University and lives with her family in Marquette.

CLAUDIA DROSEN

Musician and poet Claudia Drosen is a native of Brooklyn, New York, who left behind city life and resides with her family in Marquette, located in the Upper Peninsula of Michigan, on the South shore of Lake Superior. Claudia is principal flutist in the Marquette Symphony Orchestra. She has an M.A. in Creative Writing/Poetry from Northern Michigan University, where she was a preliminary poetry reader for *Passages North,* and a B.F.A. in Flute Performance from the University of Wisconsin-Milwaukee. Her poetry has appeared in *The Poetry Society of Michigan's Peninsula Poets, Lit UP, The Driftwood Review, Lips, Water Music: The Great Lakes State Poetry Anthology, Jewish Currents,* and *Maiden Voyage.* Claudia has been accepted for a poetry residency at the Ragdale Foundation in Lake Forest, IL. She is also a member of the band *Radio On*, a group comprised of both classical and rock musicians who combine original musical compositions and poetry. Claudia is a serious proponent of frequent and unbridled laughter.

RONNIE FERGUSON

Ronnie Ferguson is an MFA candidate and an instructor in the English department at Northern Michigan University. He has presented his scholarly and creative work internationally. A King Chavez Parks Fellow and President of the Graduate Writing Association, his creative work (often hybrid) spans the genres of poetry, music, film, theatre, and the visual arts. STREAKING IN TONGUES, the music project he shares with his son, has released several critically-acclaimed albums, most recently *Christmas with Bigfoot* with two-time U.P. Poet Laureate Marty Achatz. Their music videos have premiered on *The Hollywood Digest, Daily Pop News, Spirit You All,* and *Deep Cutz*. Their experimental music film Three Little Prayers is forthcoming. Through his work in film, Ronnie has garnered multiple awards for screenwriting and acting. His forthcoming documentaries—*Reflections of an American Sunrise, Bigfoot and Marty*, and *3-Day Novice*— explore the writing life and feature readings and interviews with various poets, including current U.S. Poet Laureate Joy Harjo. Beginning as an undergrad, he worked for a decade in the theatre, directing productions of such Pulitzer Prize-winning classics as *A Streetcar Named Desire* and *The Young Man from Atlanta*, as well as the award-winning multimedia play *The Edie and Elmira Show*, and numerous premiers. He is also the publisher of the indie platform *Harvard Square Press* and the founder of *Electric Words and Music*—a monthly series highlighting talented writers and musicians. Along with other poets, he co-founded and co-organized *The International 3-Day Poetry Chapbook Contest* and *The Great Lakes Poetry Festival*. In *Other News*, his first chapbook, was published by *Pyre Publishing* in 2021. Through the Joy Center in Ishpeming, Michigan, he leads a monthly poetry workshop on Zoom entitled *Flying Kites*. A native of Flint, Michigan, Ronnie enjoys living in Marquette and exploring the endless wonder of Michigan's Upper Peninsula.

LISA FOSMO

Lisa Fosmo is a poet and writer who resides in Escanaba and is a native of the Upper Peninsula. She enjoys spending time at her cabin in Marquette county. Lisa combines her great love of nature with her love of writing, and photography. She is a member of the Marquette poet circle, and also a member of The Poetry Society of Michigan. She has been published in Walloon Writers review, as well as anthologies and other publications in the US and abroad. In her spare time native bee conservation and habitat continue to be a passion near to her heart.

TROY GRAHAM

Troy Graham is a poet, musician and songwriter from Marquette, MI and enjoys writing poetry and conducting workshops along with musical performances. His newest work is called, "Fresh Water Mermaids" and is a read with laugh out loud humor and break-your-heart honesty. Troy has been avidly writing poems most of his adult life and travels around playing music and reading poetry at libraries.

GENEAN GRANGER

Genean Granger graduated from Kingsford High School in 1961. She was a life-long learner. She graduated from Bay College in 1969, went on to obtain her ADN from Bay, then her BSN from Northern Michigan University. She returned to NMU to pursue her dream of writing poetry and graduated with a Master's in English in May 2014. Through her Master's in English, she found a second career in Poetry. Through NMU and Sigma Tau Delta, the International English Honor Society, she participated and won a first in Original Poetry in New Orleans and was the winner of the 90th Anniversary Convention Theme. She went on to see her poems published and won numerous awards. December 2018 her book of poetry was published: *american bandstand, slices of life, and other poems.*

ALEX VARTAN GUBBINS

A poet, educator, translator of Arabic and Armenian poetry, Alex Vartan Gubbins considers the UP his home. He loves writing and spending time with his one-year old son, Niko, who is the first of the family to be born in the UP. The poem, "Inside the Forest," plays with the Anishinaabemowin's sound *"ing,"* which means "the place of..." When Alex composed the poem, he was living near the Escanaba river in Ishpeming, which means "the place up high" or "the high place." Two of the poems in this collection first appeared on WNMU, an NPR affiliate: https://www.wnmufm.org/programs/2020-05-01/national-poetry-month-alex-vartan-gubbins-pt-2

JOHN GUBBINS

John Gubbins fly fishes and writes in the Upper Peninsula of Michigan. He and his wife Carol live alongside the Middle Branch of the Escanaba River near the town of Ishpeming. They have two sons, James, a mural artist who lives in Madison, Wisconsin, and their son Alexander, a poet who writes and teaches in Dearborn, Michigan.

KATHLEEN M. HEIDEMAN

Kathleen M. Heideman is the author of *Psalms of the Early Anthropocene* (Winter Cabin Books), and a past recipient of the Marquette Arts & Culture Center's "Outstanding Writer" award. Her work has appeared in *Arcadia, Passages North, South Dakota Review, Steam Ticket, Stoneboat,* and elsewhere. Heideman completed artist residencies with the National Park Service, watersheds, scientific research stations, private foundations, and the National Science Foundation's *Antarctic Artists & Writers Program.* She is drawn to wild and threatened places, and works to defend them.

JOHN HILDEN

John Hilden is an inveterate scribbler from way back, having picked up the habit as a green apple of nineteen. He's in extra innings now and still scratching away. He's on the seventh floor and still looking up.

TARA CHANNTELLE HILL

Tara Channtelle Hill is a mother, poet, and graduate from Northern Michigan University. She has been published in *Emerge*, *MadHat Lit*, *Glass*, *Amethyst Arsenic*, *Virgogray Press* and featured in Carcinogenic Poetry's 'Top Ten Most Read List'. Tara lives in Marquette Michigan and wishes she were married to Richard Hugo (if he were alive) or someone like him.

STEWART HAKOLA

Stewart Hakola Is a father, friend, lawyer, and amateur poet who is in love with Marquette & the Copper Country.

ME KILPATRICK

ME Kilpatrick resides in Marquette, Michigan, where he serves as Coordinator of Spiritual Care and Volunteer Services at UP Health System – Marquette, and is a member of the Birmingham (AL) Friends Meeting of the Religious Society of Friends (Quaker).

JESSE KOENIG

Jesse Koenig is ___________. You can buy his book, *Brief Perversions*, if you want.

L. GAIL MAHAN

L. Gail Mahan has always loved to be out in nature. As a child growing up in Michigan most of her childhood, however, about the first five years her parents lived in Texas. Therefore, she did have some memories of her Uncle and his Ranch near Waxahachie, Texas. That sparked her curiosity enough to be adventuresome and move to the Southwest for approximately fifteen years. She wandered into the desert and explored Arches National Park as well as Mesa Verde and areas along the Colorado River area. Some of her poetry has been inspired by nature but she also has a curiosity about People and their early and unusual circumstances of death. Her Marilyn poem is one example of her poetry inspired by the mystery surrounding Marilyn's early demise. Being a musician she also loves to dance and play the Alto Sax. Rarely she chances to write about dancing but the Summoning Spring challenge gave her the inspiration to create a poem around the dance and joy one feels when inspired by a song lifting your spirits and carrying you away to the spiritual realm if only for a moment!

MATT MAKI

Matt Maki studied at Northern Michigan University and the University of Alabama; has served on the editorial boards of *Passages North*, *Black Warrior Review*, and *greatest lakes review*; founded the Marquette Poets Circle; and currently lives in Kyiv, Ukraine.

GALA MALHERBE

Gala Malherbe lives in Marquette, Michigan with her family where she spends as much time outside as she can—running, skiing, hiking, gardening, bird-watching, backpacking and sitting still. She enjoys writing about the natural world and the complex and unique experiences of being human.

BEVERLY MATHERNE

Author of six bilingual books of poetry, *Bayou des Acadiens / Blind River* the latest, is professor emerita of English at Northern Michigan University, where she served as director of the Master of Fine Arts program in creative writing, director of the Visiting Writers Program, and poetry editor of *Passages North* literary magazine. Winner of seven first-place prizes, including the Hackney Literary Award for Poetry, she has also received four Pushcart Prize nominations. She is widely published, most recently in peer-reviewed *Verbal Art: A Global Journal Devoted to Poets and Poetry*, 2021, and in *Universal Oneness: An Anthology of Magnum Opus Poems from around the World* (360 poems from 360 poets from 60 countries), 2020. With Samuel Beckett, Vladimir Nabokov, and five other writers, she is the subject of bilingual writing in a completed doctoral dissertation from the University of Paris III. Currently, she is completing a new book and restoring her Victorian home, the historic Butler House, in Ishpeming.

ROSLYN ELENA McGRATH

Marquette, Michigan resident, Roslyn Elena McGrath looks for the rhythm, rhyme, and magic in her life and written, visual, and healing work. She is the publisher of *Health & Happiness U.P. Magazine*, a supporter of self-actualization at Empowering Lightworks, and the author/illustrator of three card decks and six books, the most recent being her first book of poetry, *Sizzle, Soar, Glow, Roar: Earth Pulse Arias*. You can learn more at EmpoweringLightworks.com.

CAROLYN McMANIS

Carolyn McManis has lived in Marquette, Michigan since 1995. Now retired she enjoys swimming, reading and cooking as well as skiing and golfing with her husband, Tom. She finds inspiration for her poetry in family, emotion, and current events.

ELLA MIDDLETON

Ella Middleton is a poet, dancer, and artist, currently located in Marquette. She is originally from the Twin Cities area. Ella trained in ballet at Central Pennsylvania Youth Ballet and danced with Ballet CoLabrotory in Saint Paul, MN.

SUSAN A. MORGAN

Susan Morgan is a native Michigander, transplanted by choice to U.P. forests in 1985. A graduate of Kalamazoo College, Morgan earned a MA in Asian Studies from the University of Michigan and an MFA in Creative Non-fiction from Northern Michigan University. She retired from NMU in 2018 as Assistant Director of International Education/Study Abroad. Her poetry is informed by hours spent in trees and on the water.

JANE PIIRTO

Jane Piirto, Ph.D. is a Finnish American native of Ishpeming. Her best-known local book, *A Location the Upper Peninsula* (Sampo Publishing), is available in local libraries and on Kindle. Northern Michigan University awarded her a B.A. and an Honorary Doctor of Humane Letters. Now retired as a Trustees' Distinguished Professor from Ashland University, she worked for 53 years as an educator at various universities and school districts in Michigan, Ohio, South Dakota, and New York. She is an award-winning scholar and literary author, with 20 books and chapbooks, including Individual Artist Fellowships from the Ohio Arts Council in poetry and in fiction. She is listed as both a poet and a writer in the *Directory of American Poets & Writers*.

ROBERT POLZIN

Bob Polzin is an array of contradictions that propel him forward, mostly by walking, but sometimes by writing.

JANEEN PERGRIN RASTALL

Janeen Pergrin Rastall is the author of *In the Yellowed House* (dancing girl press, 2014), *Objects May Appear Closer* (Celery City Chapbooks, 2015) and co-author of *Heart Radicals* (About Editions, 2018) and *True Companions* (Gordon Publications, 2017). Her poems have been published in *Atticus Review, The Fourth River, North Dakota Quarterly,* and *The Raleigh Review.* She has been nominated for Best of the Net Awards and Pushcart Prizes. She is the 2021 winner of the City of Marquette Writer of the Year Award.

RICHARD J. RASTALL

Richard J. Rastall is married to the poet Janeen Pergrin Rastall. They live in Gordon, Michigan. He has an undergraduate degree and a master degree in science (mathematics) from Michigan State University. He graduated from the Thomas M. Cooley Law School and has a master of laws (in taxation) from New York University. He is the author of *Ice Volcanoes, 3rd Ed.,* (Gordon Publications, 2016). He is the co-author with Janeen Pergrin Rastall of the chapbooks *Romancing The Geek* (Gordon Publications, 2013) and *True Companions* (Gordon Publications, 2017). He co-wrote with Janeen Pergrin Rastall the play *Romancing The Geek* which premiered in 2014. He was the co-recipient with Janeen Pergrin Rastall of the City of Marquette Arts Culture Center's Community Arts Activist Award for 2017. He is the editor of *Maiden Voyage* (Gordon Publications, 2017) and *Superior Voyage* (Gordon Publications, 2022).

HELEN HASKELL REMIEN

Helen Haskell Remien lives in Ishpeming with her husband Cam where she writes, teaches yoga/creativity workshops, is the proprietor of Joy Center and plays daily in the great outdoors.

BERT RIESTERER

A native of Detroit, Bert Riesterer (1935-2018) taught both European Intellectual and German History at Indiana University, finding his true calling when he retired to Marquette, MI. The awe-inspiring experience of raw, untamed stretches of the Lake Superior shore and surrounding woods was truly transformative for him, the culmination of a lifelong spiritual journey from philosophy to poetry. He was also an avid gardener all his life.

CHRISTINE SAARI

Writer and visual artist, grew up on an Austrian mountain farm and has lived in Marquette, MI since 1971. There she worked initially as a freelance journalist for European and American sources and later took up photography. In 2011 she published a memoir *Love and War at Stag Farm: The Story of Hirschengut, an Austrian Mountain Farm 1938-1948,* which covers the formative years of her childhood during WWII. Her poetry book *Blossoms in the Dark of Winter,* inspired by her membership in The Marquette Poets Circle, was released in 2018. It deals with her European heritage and four generations of family relationships. Her major body of work as a visual artist, *Family Album*, comprised of mixed media work based on family letters, photographs, documents and artifacts, created in Marquette and exhibited in the Midwest, is now installed in the private Gallery in the Hayloft at the Austrian farm. For the past few years, she has been primarily working on an upcycle project, creating cigar box shrines from found and discarded objects. Saari is a member of The Marquette Poets Circle, The Gallery (the Marquette Artist Collective) and has a studio at Wintergreen Hills Gallery. Her poems have appeared in *Maiden Voyage, the UP Reader, Water Music and Me as a Child Poetry Series).*

REBECCA TAVERNINI

Rebecca Tavernini grew up in the U.P. She is publications director at Northern Michigan University. She has been involved in editing such books as *Voice on the Water: Great Lakes Native America Now* and *Northern Border: History and Lore of Michigan's Upper Peninsula.* Her articles have appeared in various magazines. She writes poetry on a typewriter at camp.

JOHN TAYLOR

John Taylor was born in Caro, Michigan in 1983. He was diagnosed as being on the Autism spectrum in 1991 and has been an advocate for disability rights for much of his adult life, serving on the boards of several non-profit organizations. John's poetry and fiction have appeared in the *Marquette Monthly*, the *Mythic Circle*, *The Dieselpunk E-Pulp Showcase Vol. 2.*, and *Maiden Voyage* by Gordon publications. He has also written audio narrations for several YouTube channels. He is the author of *Liber Dulcis Dolorum: the Book of Sweet Sorrows*, a collection of his poetry. John and Miriam Taylor were married in 2011 and reside in Marquette with Miriam's rabbit, Trixie.

MIRIAM TAYLOR

Miriam Taylor (Black)was born to American parents in Weston-Super Mare, Somerset, England in 1985. She attended St. John's academy and resided in England until 2004. A lifelong humanitarian, Miriam has done volunteer work for organizations such as Superior Alliance for Independent Living, Clubhouse International, and National Alliance on Mental Illness (NAMI). She is the author of "A Declaration of Love" published in England in 2003, and her poems and essays have appeared in various independent publications and newsletters in both the U.S. and U.K.

RUSSELL THORBURN

Russell Thorburn is a recipient of a National Endowment Fellowship and the first poet laureate of the Upper Peninsula of Michigan. He lives in Marquette, where he sometimes performs with his sextet Radio On. His one-act play of a retro-alternate reality, *Gimme Shelter*, was set for a premiere at the Black Box Theatre but was cancelled by the pandemic.

Index of Titles